PRINT'S BEST LOGOS & SYMBOLS 4

Copyright© 1995
by RC Publications, Inc.
All rights reserved.
Published by RC Publications, Inc.
104 Fifth Avenue
New York, NY 10011

No part of this publication may be
reproduced or used in any form or
by any means—graphic, electronic,
or mechanical, including
photocopying, recording, taping or
information storage or retrieval
systems—without written
permission from the publisher.

Manufactured in Singapore.

PRINT'S BEST LOGOS & SYMBOLS 4

Library of Congress Catalog Card Number 89-091068
ISBN 1-883915-02-3

RC PUBLICATIONS

President and Publisher: Howard Cadel
Vice President and Editor: Martin Fox
Creative Director: Andrew Kner
Managing Director, Book Projects: Linda Silver
Administrative Assistant: Nancy Silver
Assistant Art Director: Michele L. Trombley
Art Assistant: Jennifer Snipes

Margaret Richardson, who
wrote the introduction to this
volume, is editor of U&lc
magazine. She co-authored
*Print Casebooks 8: The Best in
Covers & Posters*.

Print's Best

LOGOS & SYMBOLS 4

WINNING DESIGNS FROM PRINT MAGAZINE'S NATIONAL COMPETITION

Edited by
LINDA SILVER

Introduction by
MARGARET RICHARDSON

Designed by
ANDREW KNER

Published by
**RC PUBLICATIONS, INC.
NEW YORK, NY**

A symbol is a representation of something which can't be seen, and its effectiveness is based on its appropriateness and universality. Not so long ago, a recognizable symbol might be a winged horse, and the world would have known that this was Pegasus who signified creative inspiration according to Greek myth. Is Pegasus a recognizable image anymore?

Symbols now are much more specific and much more complex, since what symbols must often represent are the accelerated transformations in technology, services, lifestyles, and products. When a company is selling interactive multimedia creative services, how can that be captured in an icon that is recognizable and effective? What images best portray the social and stylistic nuances of contemporary coffee culture? The constant challenge for designers is to invent an iconography that creates a new mythology, one that incorporates the past (albeit in historical references to recent design periods like the '50s, '60s, and '70s) while adding to the visual vocabulary of the present and future.

Logos are surely simpler to interpret. Using name brands and often explanatory tag words must ease the burden of creating an identity—or so it would seem. But think of Microsoft, a billion-dollar company associated with operating systems, software products, and now tools for accessing the Internet. Does the name Microsoft in itself capture all of these areas of development? Is Windows95 a self-explanatory identity?

What is salutary in this collection of symbols and logos, all of which appeared in recent editions of PRINT's Regional Design Annual, is the effectiveness of design in interpreting and explaining complex contemporary businesses, quite often including the business of design itself.

For example, designer/illustrator Mark Anderson of EAT Design creates a symbol using a line illustration of a tray with bottle, wine glass, grapes and wedges for a health-conscious restaurant consultant. It is simple, clean and easily identifiable (page 12). For an identity program for the Armed Forces Retirement Community, Martin Stevers designed and illustrated a formal interlocking of houses and the American flag in dramatic red, white and blue, a design that captures a sense of dignity, duty, and patriotism within the context of the social issue of retirement communities (page 184). For the Special Olympics World Games, Peter Good pays tribute to the cutout Matisse assemblages in his main image and graphically parlays these into subsidiary symbols for all of the games (pages 50, 51).

There are two notable trends revealed here in logo designs. The first is a joyous pastiche of recent graphic influences. For example, Rassman Design creates a striking illustrative logo for American Maid that is classic

CONTENTS

Americana (page 58), and Wilcox Design Atlanta simulates a bourbon label for an identity for Jeff Daniels Advertising (page 58). The person having the most fun with irreverent treatments of '50s and '60s imagery is Douglas Eymer, who art directs and illustrates a wacky family crest and two self-promotional stickers, all perfect reincarnations of type and images from the tacky past (pages 56, 57).

A noticeable typographic trend is the use of interpretive script fonts or calligraphic renderings. These are personal and contemporary and antithetical to high-tech imagery. For a clothing line from a surf shop, Scott Mires goes fully grunge with illustrator Gerald Bustamente in creating Full Bore (page 75). Art Chantry reworks the name Estrus in funky, retro and contemporary styles for Estrus Records (page 148). For Ristorante Ecco, Jennifer Morla uses a hand-lettered type evoking the rustic ambiance of the restaurant (page 16).

Occasionally, a symbol or logo captures the concept so perfectly that any other treatment would seem inappropriate, churlish even. For a promotional identity for the Minnesota Zoo's special insect and anthropod exhibit, designer/illustrator Bruce Edwards of Rapp Collins Communications cumulatively achieves the desired effect. The device is bugs, both image and word, and it is maximized on billboards advertising the show, with the reverse "bugs" logo featured in all other exhibit artifacts (page 46).

And how can the ubiquitous symbols of coffee get reinvented one more time? At least three different ways. For Verlaine coffee house, Eisenberg and Associates provides a promotional symbol resembling the cup, the curl of steam, and calligraphic flourishes done by designer/illustrator Bruce Wynne-Jones (page 42). For Java Jones, a real man's coffee, Glynn Powell places an image of an international adventurer in the cup along with the steam, while the cup rests on a strong type treatment (page 43). And Marcia Herrmann uses hot California colors and vivid illustrative type for L.A. Java gourmet coffee (page 42).

The artistry of symbol and logo design is in its compactness. It is micro-design. A symbol or logo not only has to create a first impression, it must convey a lasting impression. When a symbol becomes an icon, it adds to the symbiology of our time. When a logo becomes instantly identifiable, it becomes part of the unconscious as well as of the everyday world. A symbol or a logo design is judged immediately: remember it or it is forgotten. View the ones shown in this book from that perspective. —*Margaret Richardson*

The pulsating line represents the audio signal of Indianapolis' premier Christian talk radio station. The outline of a dove at the end of the signal depicts the message of the Holy Spirit being sent across the air waves.
DESIGN FIRM: Jensen Designs, Indianapolis, Indiana
ART DIRECTOR/ DESIGNER: Larry Jensen
BUDGET: Design: $700 (logo), $2050 (corporate identity); printing: $2164 (letterheads, business cards, and #10 envelopes)
PRINTING PROCESS: 1- and 2-color offset + blind embossing

WBRI Radio

A memorable, friendly identity for a small Phoenix-based bookstore. An owl was chosen as a symbol of scholarly wisdom and, in a whimsical way, the owl appears to be hooting the store's name.
DESIGN FIRM: Kiku Obata & Company, St. Louis, Missouri
ART DIRECTOR/ DESIGNER/ILLUSTRATOR: Richard Nelson
PRODUCTION: Teresa Norton

Houle Books

An eagle was chosen as a symbol of this air freight company's leadership position, and the bird's posture—swooping down as if about to grasp some food—suggests an aggressive business approach.

DESIGN FIRM:

Eisenberg and Associates, Dallas, Texas

CREATIVE DIRECTOR:

Arthur Eisenberg

DESIGNER/ILLUSTRATOR:

Bruce Wynne-Jones

PRINTING PROCESS:

1-color

Zeagle

This symbol is for an interactive learning center located in the Children's Zoo, where children learn how to choose, care for, and love pets.

DESIGN FIRM:

Eisenberg and Associates, Dallas, Texas

ART DIRECTOR/

DESIGNER/ILLUSTRATOR:

Tiffany Taylor

BUDGET: Design/printing:

Donated

SPCA of Texas/The Dallas Zoo

DSI

The logo suggests the protection offered by this software escrow company, which stores and maintains proprietary software and codes.

DESIGN FIRM: The Kottler Caldera Group, Phoenix, Arizona

BUDGET: Design: $12,000; printing: $10,000 (stationery package)

PRINTING PROCESS: 2-color printing with multi-level embossing

This logo was used for a conference in Yokohama, Japan, sponsored by this international business education organization for corporate presidents under the age of 50. It uses the bridge between the very Western Yokohama and the more traditional Tokyo to depict the conference's theme, "A Bridge to Understanding."

DESIGN FIRM: Tom Hair Marketing Design, Houston, Texas
ART DIRECTOR: Tom Hair
DESIGNERS: Bea Garcia, Mike Fisher
APPLICATION DESIGNER: Jan Bryza
BUDGET: Design: $2500
PRINTING PROCESS: Flat color, offset

YOKOHAMA UNIVERSITY

Young Presidents Organization

A depiction of the
recycling process of Texas
Industries' fuels program
for heating kilns in the
making of cement. The
three circles represent
liquid fuels, kiln fire, and a
balanced ecosystem.

DESIGN FIRM:
Tom Hair Marketing
Design, Houston, Texas

ART DIRECTOR: Tom Hair

DESIGNER/ILLUSTRATOR:

Yvette Hunt

BUDGET: Design: $2500

PRINTING PROCESS:

4-color

Texas Industries

Identity for a new line of
low-fat Mexican food made
with fresh ingredients.

DESIGN FIRM:
Mires Design, Inc.,
San Diego, California

ART DIRECTOR/

DESIGNER: John Ball

BUDGET: $2500

PRINTING PROCESS:

3 match colors

Rubios Restaurants, Inc. (Mexican Fast-Food Chain)

The three icons represent concepts presented in Agridyne's annual report—the protection of the neem leaf, the partnerships formed in the company's business relationships, and the harvesting of the neem leaf. The icons provide a simple contrast to other illustration and photography in the book.

DESIGN FIRM:
Arrowood Design, Salt Lake City, Utah

ART DIRECTOR/ ILLUSTRATOR:
Scott Arrowood

DESIGNERS:
Scott Arrowood, Jill Bustamante, Julia LaPine/Hornall Anderson Design Works

BUDGET: Design: $1500 (icons only)

PRINTING PROCESS:
4-color + PMS match

Agridyne (Environment-Friendly Pesticide Producer)

This mark distinguishes M.G. Swing from the competition in an extemely competitive industry.

DESIGN FIRM:
Mires Design, Inc., San Diego, California

ART DIRECTOR/ DESIGNER:
Michael Brower

ILLUSTRATOR:
Tracy Sabin

BUDGET: Design: $5000; printing: $1000

PRINTING PROCESS:
1 PMS thermography, silkscreened T-shirts, enamel paint on trucks

M. G. Swing Company (Residential/Commercial Painting)

11

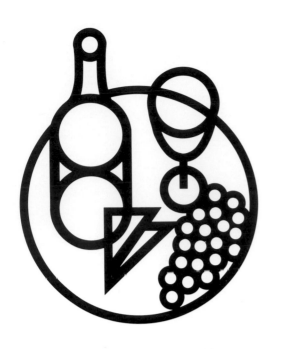

Symbol identifies menu items that are healthy or "lite" and supports the image of a health-conscious restaurant consultant.
DESIGN FIRM: EAT Design, Kansas City, Missouri

ART DIRECTOR/ DESIGNER/ILLUSTRATOR: Mark Anderson
PRINTING PROCESS: 1-color silkscreen, 4-color silkscreen and lithography

Culinary Concepts

Logo for the Greater Chicago Food Depository's long-term planning division, which works with growers and distributors to set aside fresh produce for Chicago's hungry.
DESIGN FIRM: Essex Two, Chicago, Illinois
ART DIRECTOR/ DESIGNER/ILLUSTRATOR: Joseph Michael Essex

Greater Chicago Food Depository

12

Dan Hola, Inc. (Active Wear Manufacturer)

Used on hang tags, labels, and print advertising, the logo signifies the Polynesian origin of this clothing line. "Tupenū" is a Tongan word that means skirt.
DESIGN FIRM:
Arrowood Design,
Salt Lake City, Utah
ART DIRECTOR/
DESIGNER: Scott Arrowood
BUDGET: During concept development, the designer was a partner in the clothing company and designed in trade for clothing.

Identity for a partnership of massage therapists with a holistic approach— seeing the total life benefit of their practice.
DESIGN FIRM:
Tom Hair Marketing

Design, Houston, Texas
ART DIRECTOR: Tom Hair
DESIGNER/ILLUSTRATOR:
Mike Fisher
BUDGET: Design: $2500

Body Tech (Massage Therapy for Life Enhancement)

for Efficiency,
for Beauty
for Imagination
for Creation

AF

for inspiration (rather) take one with wings

You and The FDA

The FDA recently published long-awaited and extensively revised labeling laws. The result is clearer ingredients listings on all consumer products. The former, more liberal parameters allowed claims of "low fat," "healthy" and "light" to abound; these attributes can no longer be made without meeting strict requirements. The major areas affected are:

Serving Sizes now standardized to common portions, rather than left to the producer's choice.

Nutritional Information: an expanded back panel box with a more detailed ingredient breakdown, expressed as a percentage of a recommended 2,000 calorie per day diet.

Descriptors: Low fat—for foods with less than 3 grams of fat per serving. Fat Free—contains only one-half gram or less per serving.

Light—used only for foods that contain at least one-third fewer calories than the company's regular product.

Calorie-free or No Calories —any product with less than five calories.

Low Cholesterol—contains 20 mg. or less per serving and per 100 grams of food, and contains 2 grams or less of saturated fat per serving.

All of this can be found in greater detail in the FDA's 1000 page report on Labeling Law No. P893-139905, which can be obtained by contacting the National Technical Information Service at 703 487 4650.

Design One is a partnership that believes in listening to our clients. We create brand and corporate identities, packaging design and a wide variety of print materials. Our constant goal is to communicate with clarity, precision and distinctive visual appeal.

For more information about what we do, please call James Fash, Jacqueline Ghosin, or Franz Platte at 415 954 0710.

Our clients include:
Ballard, Biehl & Kaiser
Bank of America
Bank of A. Levy
California Transplant Donor Network
Dreyer's Grand Ice Cream
Information Access Company
Nissin Foods
Norwest Bank
Regional Organ Procurement Agency of Southern California
St. Mary's Hospital
Seagate Technology
Tastemaker
Uncle Grant's Foods
World Presidents' Organization

*Design One
The Roundhouse Plaza
1500 Sansome Street, Suite 204
San Francisco, California 94111
Telephone 415 954 0710*

Bigger is Bigger, Not Always Better

Today, most companies are leaner than ever before. Managers are held accountable for the results of their projects, and smaller budgets need to go much further. Business decisions now are made differently than they were just a few years ago. It's no longer considered a wise choice to simply hire the biggest because "they're the safest bet." One has to justify any decision with reason and objectivity. Among the people who hire design firms, conversations inevitably arise about assigning a project to a small firm. Their questions address service, quality, creativity and budget. Several factors make small firms the logical alternative to large ones.

More Personal and Immediate Service—The people you talk to at small firms own the businesses they represent. Because of this, it is in their interest to address your issues as well as, if not better than, a large firm. Owners provide exceptional service to customers because their livelihood and future depend on it. And with frequent and personal attention, your project isn't lost among the crowd. In large firms, it's much harder to inspire that kind of motivation.

Quality and Creativity—Powerful, affordable technology has enabled creativity in even the smallest design firms to flourish. This is achieved by significantly reducing the time needed to execute ideas, leaving a lot more time devoted to the most important part of your job… *the development of ideas.* Years ago at least 30% of a project's time was reserved for producing presentation materials. Now maybe only 10% is needed. Secondly, although the creative aspect of a project is the most visible, the refinement and production of the chosen concept is always the make-or-break part. Technology makes huge savings available through fast and easy changes which previously took weeks to do.

Budget—Although cost should not be the sole reason for your choice of firms, it is an influencing factor. You need to feel confident that the firm you choose understands your needs and has the skills to do the job. But if a small firm has the right experience and offers the service you want, if the work is thoughtful and imaginative, then why pay more for it? Small firms are simply not burdened with unnecessary overhead, and you are not burdened with the price.

Design One is a partnership that believes in listening to our clients. We create brand and corporate identities, packaging design and a wide variety of print materials. Our constant goal is to communicate with clarity, precision and distinctive visual appeal.

For more information about what we do, please call James Fash, Jacqueline Ghosin, or Franz Platte at 415 954 0710.

Our clients include:
Ballard, Biehl & Kaiser
Bank of A. Levy
Bank of America
California Transplant Donor Network
Charles Schwab & Co.
Dreyer's Grand Ice Cream
Golden Brands Marketing
Information Access Company
Job Parilux
Macromedia
Nissin Foods
Norwest Bank
Pacific Gear Products
Pacific Telesis Group
Regional Organ Procurement Agency of Southern California
Seagate Technology
Tastemaker
Trinity Ventures
Uncle Grant's Foods
VISA U.S.A.
World Presidents' Organization

Design One, The Roundhouse Plaza, 1500 Sansome Street, Suite 204, San Francisco, California 94111, Telephone 415 954 0710

DESIGN FIRM: Design One, San Francisco, California

ART DIRECTOR: Jacqueline Ghosin, Jim Fash, Franz Platte

ILLUSTRATOR: Andre Francois

BUDGET: Printing: $2500 for newsletters

PRINTING PROCESS: 4-color (newsletters), 4-color + blind embossing (letterhead and collateral materials)

 &

&

Logo reflects the partners' different design styles and works on its own without copy. An imminent relocation restricted the printing budget, but by adding a different ink color and paper stock to each piece, the package appears more expensive than it was. Printing copy on a laser printer reduced overall costs.

DESIGN FIRM: Swanson & Swanson, A Design Studio, Inc., Tampa, Florida

ILLUSTRATORS: Eric Swanson, Laura Swanson

BUDGET: Printing: $500

PRINTING PROCESS: 2-color offset, different color ink and paper for each piece; cards are printed 2/2

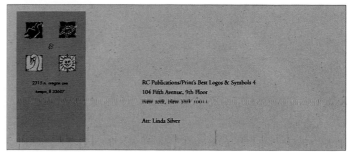

Hand-lettered type evokes the rustic Italian ambiance of this award-winning San Francisco restaurant.

DESIGN FIRM:

Morla Design, San Francisco, California

ART DIRECTOR:

Jennifer Morla

DESIGNERS/LETTERERS:

Jennifer Morla, Craig Bailey

BUDGET: In trade for food

PRINTING PROCESS:

3-color offset

Ristorante Ecco

Identity for line of business and office accessories—picture frames, business card holders, and money clips.

DESIGN FIRM:

Eymer Design, Inc., Boston, Massachusetts

ART DIRECTOR/ ILLUSTRATOR:

Douglas Eymer

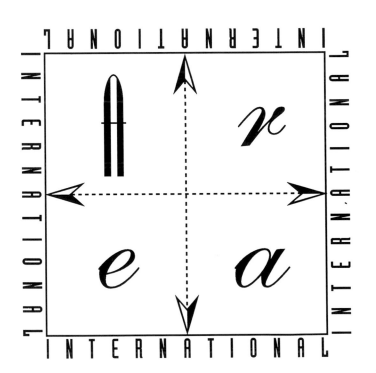

Area International

Logo communicates the speed and elegance of basketball through the letterform interpretations of a gazelle.

DESIGN FIRM:
The Kottler Caldera Group, Phoenix, Arizona
ART DIRECTORS:
Doreen Caldera,
Paul Caldera

DESIGNER:
Doreen Caldera
BUDGET: Design: $11,000;
Applications: $15,000
PRINTING PROCESS:
4-color silkscreen,
custom embroidery

Gazelle (Basketball Sportswear)

DESIGN FIRM:
Mires Design, Inc.,
San Diego, California
ART DIRECTOR/
DESIGNER: John Ball
ILLUSTRATOR:
Miguel Pérez
BUDGET: $5000
PRINTING PROCESS:
Black + a palette of four
different colors for type

California Center for the Arts, Escondido

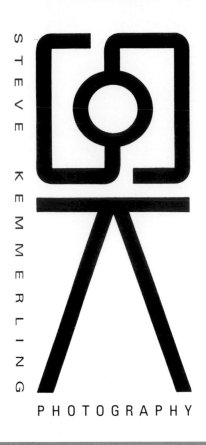

S T E V E K E M M E R L I N G

PHOTOGRAPHY

The image of a stylized 4x5 camera shows what Steve Kemmerling does, as well as who he is (his initials are formed when the mark is viewed horizontally).
DESIGN FIRM:
Brad Norr Design, Minneapolis, Minnesota
DESIGNER: Brad Norr
BUDGET: Design: in trade, printing: $500 (stationery)

Steve Kemmerling Photography (Commercial Photographer)

This image for a faculty/ student jazz club was taken from a successful fundraiser poster.
DESIGN FIRM:
Sommese Design, State College, Pennsylvania
ART DIRECTOR/ ILLUSTRATOR:
Lanny Sommese

DESIGNER:
Kristin Sommese
BUDGET: Pro bono by faculty
PRINTING PROCESS:
Silkscreen (poster)

Penn State Jazz Club

Image accompanying an article on updating Betty Crocker's image.

DESIGN FIRM:

C.S. Anderson Design Company, Minneapolis, Minnesota

ART DIRECTOR:

Charles S. Anderson

DESIGNERS:

Charles S. Anderson, Erik Johnson

ILLUSTRATOR:

Erik Johnson

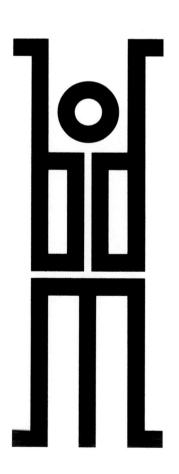

Promotional image for a fitness trainer and a line of workout clothes.

DESIGN FIRM:

Mires Design, Inc., San Diego, California

ART DIRECTOR:

Michael Brower

BUDGET: $6500

PRINTING PROCESS:

Silkscreen (garments), offset (letterhead package)

Bod•E Precision

The identity for this restaurant serving Southwestern cuisine features illustrations derived from Southwestern Indian art.
DESIGN FIRM: EAT Design, Kansas City, Missouri
ART DIRECTOR/
DESIGNER:
Patrice Eilts-Jobe
ILLUSTRATORS:
Rachel Eilts, Carly Harter
PRINTING PROCESS:
Silkscreened on real bark paper (logo)

PB&J Restaurants (Restaurant Owners)

Liza

Promotional logo for a chair design.
DESIGN FIRM:
Michael Orr + Associates, Inc., Corning, New York
ART DIRECTOR:
Michael Orr
DESIGNERS:
Gregory Duell, Douglas Prickett
PRINTING PROCESS:
4-color + 2 varnish

The Gunlocke Company (Furniture Manufacture/Design)

20

Corporate identity for a manufacturer of cosmetic and jewelry organizers. The arched lines of the letterforms suggest the antlers of the African antelope from which the company takes its name. These black lines, like the product, organize the colored shapes into patterns.

DESIGN FIRM: B-LIN, San Diego, California

ART DIRECTOR: Brian Lovell

DESIGNERS: Brian Lovell, Lisa Castillo, Vicki Wyatt

PRINTING PROCESS: 4- or 6-color (most of the pieces)

Sassaby, Inc.

Identity for a photographer
who shoots black-and-
white exclusively.
Reproductions of his work
identified with a rubber
stamp are used as
promotional pieces.

DESIGN FIRM:
Horjus Design, San Diego,
California

DESIGNER/ILLUSTRATOR:
Peter Horjus

BUDGET: Design: in trade
for photography

Byron Pepper Photography

A humorous and
memorable identity
for a photographer.
DESIGN FIRM:
Market Sights, Inc.,
Washington, DC

DESIGNER:
Marilyn Worseldine
ILLUSTRATOR:
Norman Rainock
BUDGET: Barter
PRINTING PROCESS:
Offset, black

Stan Barouh

Intended to convey a warm, down home image for a new restaurant, this charming logo was not used because it cost too much to apply it to signs and other materials.

DESIGN FIRM:
Sommese Design, State College, Pennsylvania

ART DIRECTOR/
DESIGNER/ILLUSTRATOR:
Lanny Sommese
COMPUTER DESIGNER:
Steve Ealy
BUDGET: Design: $1000

A humorous take on a well-known tale effectively communicates the exuberance of the owner of this venture business.

DESIGN FIRM:
Sol Design Team,
Redwood City, California
ART DIRECTOR:
Joan Matteucci

DESIGNERS: Steve Elmore, Matt Finnigan
BUDGET: Design: $500; printing: in trade and laser printed for a more home-spun look
PRINTING PROCESS:
Silkscreen (T-shirts); laser printed on recycled stock and colored with crayons (labels)

Jack's Roasted Nuts Company

24

Mike Davis Golf School

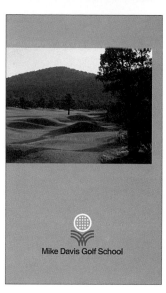

Mike Davis Golf School

This identity works well in one color (newspaper) and multicolor (embroidery, silkscreen, print).

DESIGN FIRM:
Nancy Davis Design & Illustration, Portland, Oregon

ART DIRECTOR/ DESIGNER/ILLUSTRATOR: Nancy Davis

PHOTOGRAPHER: Kristen Finnegan (brochure)

PRINTING PROCESS: PMS offset (letterhead); 4-color offset (brochure)

Penn State Golf Courses

A new symbol reflects the updated look of the redesigned golf courses, where exotic grasses serve as markers and decoration. The new mark was also used on merchandise.

DESIGN FIRM:
Penn State Design Practicomm, State College, Pennsylvania

ART DIRECTOR:
Lanny Sommese

DESIGNER/ILLUSTRATOR:
Robinson Smith

BUDGET: At cost as part of the Design Practicomm class at Penn State University. Each of nine students designed a mark, from which the final design was chosen.

Design Mirage (Interactive Multimedia System Design)

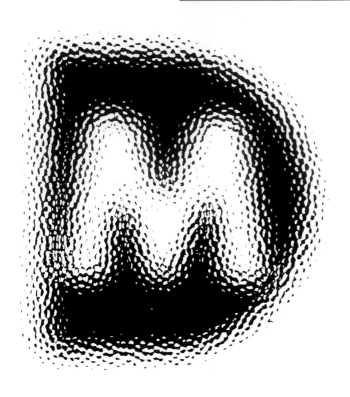

Although Design Mirage works almost exclusively with the computer, the look of its symbol was not the result of computer manipulation, but rather was derived from a high-contrast photostat of the letterforms shot through a patterned glass surface.

DESIGN FIRM: Sommese Design, State College, Pennsylvania

ART DIRECTOR/ DESIGNER: Lanny Sommese

PRINTING PROCESS: 1-color, offset

Green (Golf Instruction/Clinic)

Logo promotes a golf instruction/teaching clinic and is prominently featured on a giveaway T-shirt.

DESIGN FIRM: Scott Johnson Design, Rockford, Illinois

ART DIRECTOR/ DESIGNER: Scott Johnson

BUDGET: Printing: $500

PRINTING PROCESS: Silkscreen (T-shirts)

The logo is an example of an altered image taken from the archive.

DESIGN FIRM:
C.S. Anderson Design Company, Minneapolis, Minnesota

ART DIRECTOR:
Charles S. Anderson

DESIGNERS:
Charles S. Anderson, Erik Johnson, Paul Howalt

ILLUSTRATOR:
CSA Archive altered symbol

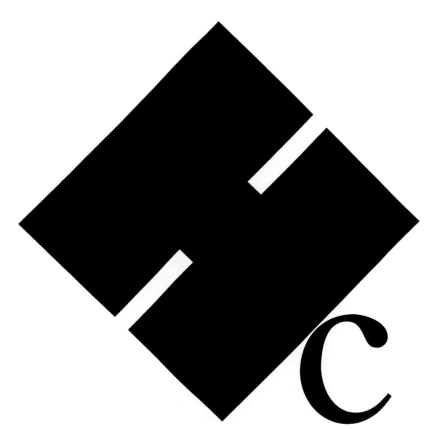

Logo for a multi-disciplinary public relations/public affairs and advertising agency.

DESIGN FIRM: Essex Two, Chicago, Illinois

ART DIRECTOR/ DESIGNER/ILLUSTRATOR:
Joseph Michael Essex

A mark for a division within this utility that is overhauling computerized customer services. Called Team Coyote, the division works outside the normal bureaucracy of the company and can therefore accomplish change more quickly.

DESIGN FIRM:
Franklin Stoorza,
San Diego, California

ART DIRECTOR:
Craig Fuller

ILLUSTRATOR:
Tracy Sabin

BUDGET: Design: $600

The logo is part of an overall marketing program designed to appeal to an audience of 3- to 20-year-olds. The bear is a universal symbol that targets all ages in a friendly manner.

DESIGN FIRM:
Jensen Designs,
Indianapolis, Indiana

ART DIRECTOR/
DESIGNER: Larry Jensen

BUDGET: Design: $700 (logo); printing: $1395 (letterhead, #10 envelope, business card)

PRINTING PROCESS:
2-color offset (stationery); silkscreen (specialty advertising)

28

Women & Horses®

Introductory logo for an organization whose focus is on increasing the awareness of services, techniques and events specifically available to women in the horse industry.

DESIGN FIRM:

TGD Communications, Alexandria, Virginia

ART DIRECTOR:

Rochelle Gray

DESIGNER: Trish Palasik

BUDGET: Design: $2500

Promotional symbol for one of the largest bowling-alley grand openings ever held in Taipei, Taiwan.

DESIGN FIRM:

United Design, Calabasas, California

ART DIRECTOR/

DESIGNER/ILLUSTRATOR:

Wen Ping Hsiao

BUDGET: $25,000

PRINTING PROCESS:

Black-and-white or 1 PMS

Dragon Bowling Center

A new identity program coordinates packaging for the various components of CTB's elementary and secondary school administrative software. The symbol also communicates the integration of the different types of software offered: class attendance tracking, library cataloging, budget and accounting, etc.

DESIGN FIRM:

Landkamer Hamer Design, San Francisco, California

DESIGNER/ILLUSTRATOR:

Mark Landkamer

BUDGET: Design: $12,000 (includes final art)

PRINTING PROCESS:

4 match colors, offset lithography

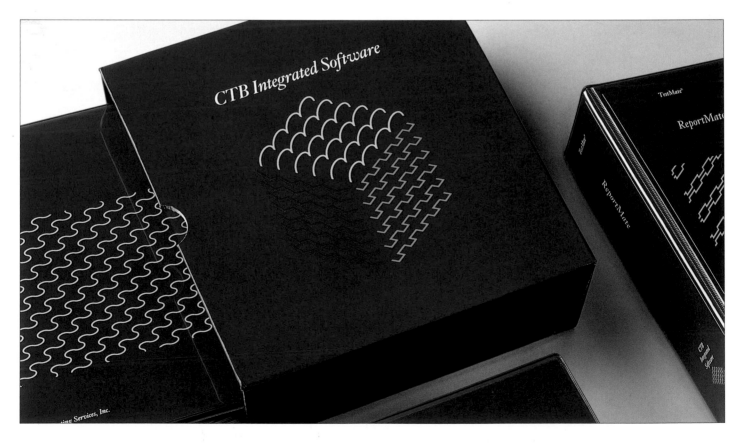

Appearing as art on the back of a book entitled *Multiple Voices in Feminist Film Criticism*, this symbol also was used on all correspondence and promotion for the book. Based on Maillol's sculpture *Seated Woman*, the black/white planes intersecting the mark allude to the varying viewpoints referred to in the book's title.

DESIGN FIRM:
Brad Norr Design,
Minneapolis, Minnesota
DESIGNER: Brad Norr

This corporate identity for a surgical group was designed by a hospital staff designer.

DESIGN FIRM:
The Graduate Hospital,
Philadelphia, Pennsylvania
ART DIRECTOR/
DESIGNER: Lynne Lyon
BUDGET: Design: $1000;
printing: $1050 per 1000
PRINTING PROCESS:
2-color

This design firm's positive outlook is represented in its logo, which also presents the design process as being flexible and continuous.

DESIGN FIRM:

Olver Dunlop Associates, Chicago, Illinois

ART DIRECTORS:

Julia Dunlop, Patty Schreiber

DESIGNER/ILLUSTRATOR:

Kara Kuster

Olver Dunlop Associates

Olver Dunlop Associates (Graphic Design)

A visual identity for a company involved in multinational and multilingual business consulting.

DESIGN FIRM:

Pattee Design, Des Moines, Iowa

ART DIRECTOR:

Steve Pattee

DESIGNERS: Steve Pattee, Kelly Stiles

PRINTING PROCESS:

Offset

Global Technology Resource Group

MOONSTRUCK

chocolatier

The experience of savoring chocolate is related in this image to the mystical effect of the moon via the dancing Pan-like figure.

DESIGN FIRM:

Sandstrom Design, Portland, Oregon

DESIGNER:

Jennifer Lyon Bartch

ILLUSTRATOR:

George Vogt

BUDGET: Design: $5000

PRINTING PROCESS:

Offset, 1 PMS + spot varnish

Moonstruck Chocolatier (Premium Chocolate Manufacturer)

CRAFT WORLD

Corporate identity appearing on company literature, including catalogs, signage, collateral.

DESIGN FIRM:

Dwight Douthit Design, Houston, Texas

ART DIRECTOR/

DESIGNER:

Dwight Douthit

ILLUSTRATOR:

Craig White

BUDGET: Design: $5000 (total package); printing: $5000

PRINTING PROCESS:

2-color lithography

CraftWorld (Arts & Crafts Mail Order)

Logo promotes the
human side of the human
resources industry.
DESIGN FIRM:
Thomas Design, San Jose,
California
ART DIRECTOR/
ILLUSTRATOR:
Craig Thomas
BUDGET: Design: $1200
(logo & stationery),
$2745 (brochure), $3665
(newsletter)
PRINTING PROCESS:
2-color (stationery),
 2-color + varnish
(brochure), 3-color
(newsletter)

This new logo repositioned
Ergodyne as a leader in the
office products market.
DESIGN FIRM:
Duffy Design, Minneapolis,
Minnesota
ART DIRECTOR/
DESIGNER/ILLUSTRATOR:
Neil Powell

Ergodyne Corporation (Workplace Health/Safety Products)

Symbol promotes aerobics instruction with a hip-hop beat.

DESIGN FIRM:

Coblyn Design, Bethesda, Maryland

ART DIRECTOR/

ILLUSTRATOR:

Chip Coblyn

BUDGET: Pro bono

PRINTING PROCESS:

1-color, offset and 600 dpi laser printer

K-Mac Aerobics

Promotional symbol for a trade association conference in Sun Valley, Idaho.

DESIGN FIRM:

Reuter Design,

San Francisco, California

ART DIRECTOR/

DESIGNER: William Reuter

ILLUSTRATOR: Jose Bila

BUDGET: Design: pro bono; printing: $500

PRINTING PROCESS:

Lithography + embossing

American Institute of Architects/Idaho Chapter

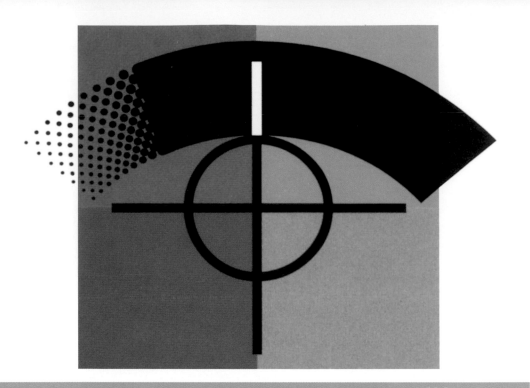

A new corporate symbol for a color separator/ prepress house projects the image of a company producing high-quality color.
DESIGN FIRM:
Whaley Design, St. Paul, Minnesota
ART DIRECTOR/
DESIGNER: Kevin Whaley
BUDGET: Design: $6000
PRINTING PROCESS:
5 match colors, offset

Lithoprep

ART DIRECTOR/
DESIGNER: Ana Pinto,
New York, New York
PRINTING PROCESS:
Offset

Optic Nerve USA, Inc. (Commercial Film Production)

This logo establishes an identity for VTIC, an information retrieval service utilizing both traditional and electronic techniques. The Center emphasizes speed and accuracy.

DESIGN FIRM:

Plaid River Design, Inc., Blacksburg, Virginia

DESIGNER:

Jennifer Goodreau

BUDGET: Design: $300 (logo); $650 (brochure design & printing)

PRINTING PROCESS: 2-color

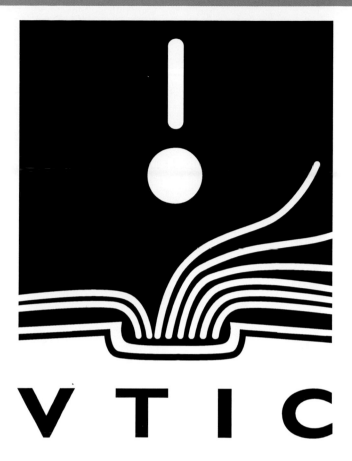

VTIC

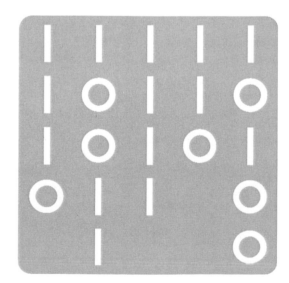

Nsoft

This trade association identity, using binary code to spell out Nsoft, is designed to generate interest and communicate excellence.

DESIGN FIRM:

Design Trust, Inc., Wilton, Connecticut

DESIGNER: David Cundy

This identity for two designers of alternative, one-of-a-kind fashion items was achieved on a shoestring budget. The low dpi is intentional to symbolize the initial rough beginnings of a small business.

DESIGN FIRM:
Patricia J. Paolella Design, Rocky River, Ohio

DESIGNER:
Patricia Paolella

LETTERERS:
Patricia Paolella, Stephanie Shields-Weber

ART DIRECTOR:
Charles Pearce

PRINTING PROCESS:
Xerox 5775 SSE color copier, TEK Phaser (Tektronix Phaser III) color printer

The Sweat Shop

Human Resources

Used by the company's Human Resources department on its internal literature, the logo plays off the overall corporate logo, which includes a square shape. The Human Resources logo incorporates the many departments and employees under the Human Resources group.

DESIGN FIRM:
Design Trust, Inc., Wilton, Connecticut

ART DIRECTOR:
David Cundy

DESIGNER:
Tracy H.M. Hubbard

Greenwich Capitol Markets, Inc. (Financial Trading/Consulting)

TECHNOLOGY

IS OUR MIDDLE NAME

Initially designed for proposed packaging, this logo was later used as a product sheet headline.

DESIGN FIRM:

Whaley Design, St. Paul, Minnesota

ART DIRECTOR/

DESIGNER: Kevin Whaley

BUDGET: Design: $2000

PRINTING PROCESS:

4-color, offset

The logo ties together the organization's cause with the headline performer's name in an elegant overall design for a promotional event.

DESIGN FIRM: May & Co., Dallas, Texas

ART DIRECTOR:

Douglas May

DESIGNER:

Candace Buchanan Morgan

BUDGET: Pro bono

PRINTING PROCESS:

4-color spot

American Foundation for AIDS Research/AmFAR)

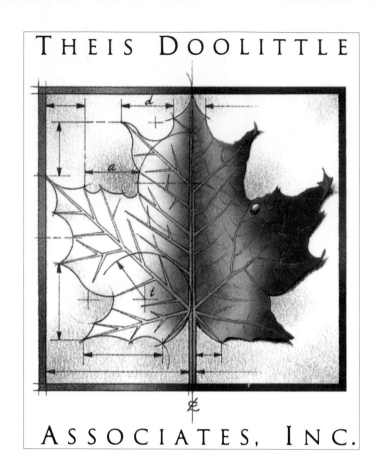

THEIS DOOLITTLE
ASSOCIATES, INC.

A new partner provided the stimulus for a fresh marketing program for this architecture/ landscape architecture firm. The identity created for this program seamlessly integrates natural and man-made forms.

DESIGN FIRM: EAT Design, Kansas City, Missouri

ART DIRECTOR/ DESIGNER:

Patrice Eilts-Jobe

ILLUSTRATOR:

Michael Weaver

PRINTING PROCESS:

4-color process for most applications or a 1-color mezzotint

Theis Doolittle Associates, Inc.

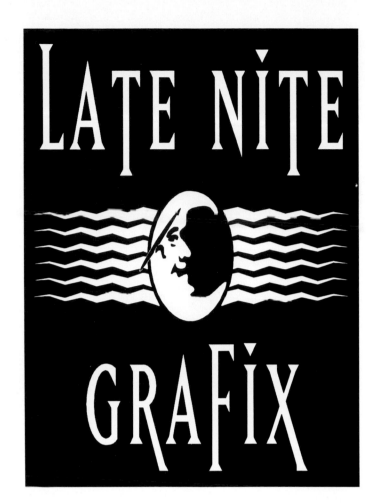

The logo update for this graphic design/advertising firm was created entirely on computer and is used in a multitude of applications.

DESIGN FIRM:

Late Nite Grafix, Sante Fe, New Mexico

DESIGNER/ILLUSTRATOR:

Gary Cascio

BUDGET: Printing: $130 (stationery), $200 (T-shirts)

PRINTING PROCESS:

1-color (stationery), silkscreen (T-shirt)

Late Nite Grafix

Promotional symbol for a
coffee house.

DESIGN FIRM:

Eisenberg and Associates,

Dallas, Texas

CREATIVE DIRECTOR:

Arthur Eisenberg

ART DIRECTOR/

DESIGNER/ILLUSTRATOR:

Bruce Wynne-Jones

PRINTING PROCESS:

Multicolor

Verlaine

For this espresso cart
coffee company, the
designers devised a bright,
bold, playful image to
appear on stationery and
product labels.

DESIGN FIRM:

Marcia Herrmann Design,
Modesto, California

DESIGNER:

Marcia Herrmann

BUDGET: Design: $1500;

printing: $1500

PRINTING PROCESS:

4-color offset (stationery),

4-color flexography

(labels)

L.A. Java

The logo for this restaurant trade association communicates the service aspect of the restaurant industry with a uniquely Hawaiian image. The modified running figure was inspired by Hawaiian petroglyphs. The border treatment around the symbol is an actual Hawaiian barkcloth pattern.

DESIGN FIRM:
Garma Graphic Design, Inc., Waipahu, Hawaii
ART DIRECTOR/
DESIGNER/ILLUSTRATOR:
Alfredo Lista Garma

Java Jones, Inc.

This unusual image projects an international flavor and sets Java Jones apart from the other coffeehouses proliferating in the area.

DESIGN FIRM:
Powell Design Office, Dallas, Texas
ART DIRECTOR/
DESIGNER/ILLUSTRATOR:
Glyn Powell
PRINTING PROCESS:
1-color

Seeking a symbol that would be both memorable and appropriate to the firm's design and business philosophy, the designers chose a crane. Besides being a wonderfully graceful, elegant creature and an apt metaphor, the crane is also a symbol of longevity and good luck. Positioning the bird as if poised for flight was meant to symbolize freedom of creative thought.

DESIGN FIRM:
Groff Creative Inc.,
Bethesda, Maryland

ART DIRECTOR:
Lauren S. Groff

DESIGNER: Jay M. Groff

BUDGET: Printing: $2562

PRINTING PROCESS:
2-color offset + foil stamp
(stationery package)

Groff Creative, Inc. (Graphic Design/Marketing Communications)

Identity for a new residential community.

DESIGN FIRM:
Dwight Douthit Design,
Houston, Texas

ART DIRECTOR:
Dwight Douthit

DESIGNERS: Jana Fritsch,
Dwight Douthit

ILLUSTRATOR:
Patty McCormick

BUDGET: Design: $10,000
(entire package); printing:
$10,000

PRINTING PROCESS:
2-color lithography

Trammell Crow Residential (Real Estate Development/Management)

44

Identity for a small boutique winery in Colorado's Vail Valley near the Eagle River.

DESIGN FIRM: Rassman Design, Denver, Colorado

DESIGNERS: Amy Rassman, John Rassman, Lyn D'Amato

E A G L E

R I V E R

W I N E R Y

The mythological phoenix rising from its ashes—a symbol of rebirth and renewal—is a meaningful icon for a youth pops orchestra that was formed as an educational program of The San Damiano Consort, a non-profit musical group.

DESIGNER/ILLUSTRATOR: John Sotirakis, Pittsburgh, Pennsylvania

PRINTER: Banksville Express, Pittsburgh, Pennsylvania (stationery)

BUDGET: Design: pro bono ($2400 value); printing: $400 (stationery)

PRINTING PROCESS: 1-color offset (stationery), white silkscreen (hats and T-shirts)

Promotional identity for the Minnesota Zoo's special summer insect and anthropods exhibit. The logo was featured in all exhibit communications, such as TV, print and outdoor billboard advertising, on-site signage, merchandise (T-shirts, hats, etc.), and food service souvenir cups, as well as in tie-in communications with Target department store.

DESIGN FIRM:
Rapp Collins
Communications,
Minneapolis, Minnesota
ART DIRECTOR/
DESIGNER/ILLUSTRATOR:
Bruce Edwards
BUDGET: Design/
production: $50,000

Minnesota Zoo

Promotional logo for the
annual picnic of the
statewide association of
pharmacy students.

DESIGN FIRM:

Dwight Douthit Design,
Houston, Texas

ART DIRECTOR/

DESIGNER:

Dwight Douthit

ILLUSTRATOR:

Craig White

BUDGET: Pro bono

PRINTING PROCESS:

Silkscreen (T-shirts)

Tri School Pharmacy

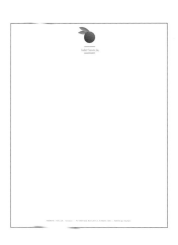

DESIGN FIRM:

JOED Design, Elmhurst,

Illinois

ART DIRECTOR/

DESIGNER: Ed Rebek

BUDGET: $6000

PRINTING PROCESS:

2-color

Herman Keller (Florida Orange Grower)

A new logo reinforces the new name for the accreditation association of American zoological parks and aquariums. The goal was to represent zoos and aquariums equally and to portray the animals within their own environments rather than on display in cages.

DESIGN FIRM:
Grafik Communications Ltd., Alexandria, Virginia
DESIGNERS: David Collins, Judy F. Kirpich, Susan English
ILLUSTRATOR:
David Collins
PRINTING PROCESS:
1-color, offset

Displayed on signs, this logo identifies areas of the city that have been adopted by civic or neighborhood groups.

DESIGN FIRM:
Dean Wilhite Design Company, Oklahoma City, Oklahoma
ART DIRECTOR/
DESIGNER: Dean Wilhite
BUDGET: Design: $1200; printing/sign stock: $1300
PRINTING PROCESS:
Offset lithography, 2-color metallic inks (certificates), silkscreen (signs)

Oklahoma City Beautiful

48

McDonald's association with this charity fundraiser is clearly communicated by the double arches in the logo.

DESIGN FIRM:

Garma Graphic Design, Inc., Waipahu, Hawaii

ART DIRECTOR/ DESIGNER/ILLUSTRATOR:

Alfredo Lista Garma

BUDGET: Pro bono

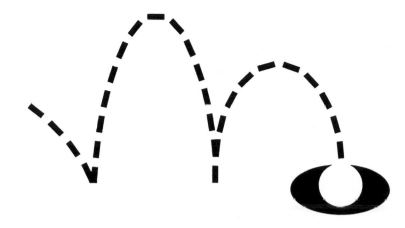

Ronald McDonald House Golf Classic

Ronald McDonald (Children's Charity)

The logo was designed to communicate an unpleasant surgical procedure in an elegant and unexpected way. The discus thrower focuses on the desired result—full range of motion without pain or discomfort.

DESIGN FIRM:

Kiku Obata & Company, St. Louis, Missouri

ART DIRECTOR:

Ed Mantels-Seeker

DESIGNERS:

Ed Mantels-Seeker, Richard Nelson

PRODUCTION:

Michael Beaudoin

PRINTING PROCESS:

4 flat colors, offset (stationery)

The Hernia Institute

Volleyball

Team Handball

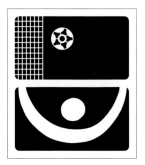

Softball

Rowing

Tennis

Table Tennis

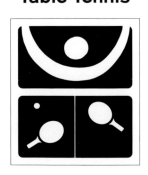

Sailing

Roller Skating

Special Olympics
World Games
Connecticut 1995

Graphic
Standards
Manual

In the symbol for the Special Olympics World Games, the simplicity of the running figure captured the essence of sports. The symbol was reproduced in print, fabric, metal, plastic and paint, in sizes ranging from 1/4" to 12'. Also shown here are some of the subsidiary symbols created for the games, the largest sports event in the world in 1995. DESIGN FIRM: Peter Good Graphic Design, Chester, Connecticut ART DIRECTOR/ DESIGNER/ILLUSTRATOR: Peter Good

Special Olympics

Powerlifting

Golf
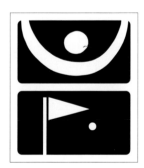

Equestrian

Croquet
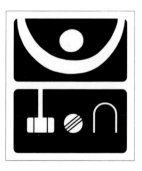

Gymnastics

Football
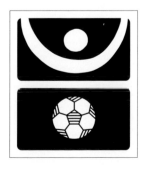

Cycling

Bowling

Identity appearing on the back of greeting cards for sale and on company stationery.
DESIGN FIRM:
Endorphin Design,
Denton, Texas
DESIGNER: Karen Dorff

Goo-Goo Greetings (Custom Birth Announcements)

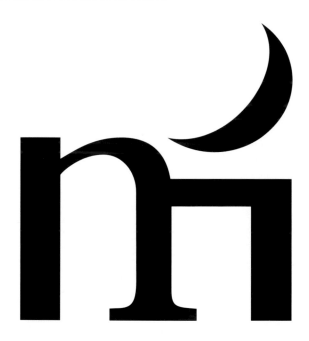

An enigmatic identity for a new furniture business owned by an artist who not only designs the furniture but creates the advertising.
DESIGN FIRM:
FORDESIGN, Alexandria, Louisiana
ART DIRECTOR/
DESIGNER: Frank Ford
METAL FABRICATOR:
Michael Ford

BUDGET: Design: pro bono; $1500 (metal fabrication and teaser mailing)
PRINTING PROCESS:
The mailer was printed on aluminum printing plates and the logo was carved by hand from 3/4" aluminum to reinforce the fact that Mirage creates metal furniture.

Mirage Furniture (Metal Furniture Design/Production)

Custom Covers (Custom Boat Covers/Awnings)

The logo is a visual
expression of fabric
covering.

DESIGN FIRM:

Peter Good Graphic Design,

Chester, Connecticut

ART DIRECTOR/

DESIGNER/ILLUSTRATOR:

Peter Good

PRINTING PROCESS:

1-color offset

Promotional logo for Janie
Stampley's merchandising
services.

DESIGN FIRM:

Eisenberg and Associates,

Dallas, Texas

CREATIVE DIRECTOR:

Arthur Eisenberg

DESIGNER/ILLUSTRATOR:

Saul Torres

BUDGET: Printing: $100

PRINTING PROCESS:

1 color

Stampley Merchandising

53

The fountain image
reinforces the idea that
this firm is *the source* for
thoroughbred horses.

DESIGN FIRM:

Tracy-Locke/DDB

Needham, Dallas, Texas

ART DIRECTOR/

ILLUSTRATOR:

Jonathan Rice

BUDGET: Design: $1000;

printing: $500

PRINTING PROCESS:

2-color offset

The Horse Source (Thoroughbred-Horse Broker)

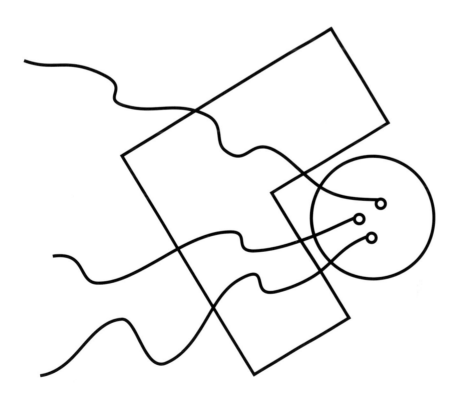

An identity that
communicates the
company's special
character: avant-garde,
quirky, specialized.

DESIGN FIRM: Pure,

Stamford, Connecticut

ART DIRECTOR/

DESIGNER/ILLUSTRATOR:

James Pettus

CONSULTANT:

James Rowley

Fabrique (Textile Design for Fashion Industry)

DESIGN FIRM:

Design Center,

Minnetonka, Minnesota

ART DIRECTOR:

John Reger

DESIGNER:

Sherwin Schwartzrock

PRINTING PROCESS:

Engraving (stationery)

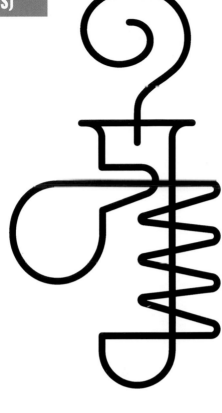

Promotional logo for a tribute to fathers, held at a shopping mall in which chamber music performances were scheduled in the midst of a Harley Davidson exhibition. The logo, symbolizing heavenly music and winged machines, was used throughout an extensive marketing program.

DESIGN FIRM:

Steven Sessions, Inc., Houston, Texas

ART DIRECTOR:

Steven Sessions

DESIGNERS: Phil Schmitt, Steven Sessions

ILLUSTRATOR:

Phil Schmitt

PRINTING PROCESS:

Offset lithography

A designer's family crest.

DESIGN FIRM:

Eymer Design, Inc.,

Boston, Massachusetts

ART DIRECTOR/

ILLUSTRATOR:

Douglas Eymer

Douglas Eymer

Symbol for a laboratory that identifies odors from locations around the world.

DESIGN FIRM:

Design Center,

Minnetonka, Minnesota

ART DIRECTOR:

John Reger

DESIGNER:

Sherwin Schwartzrock

PRINTING PROCESS:

6-color (folder), 1-color

(insert sheets)

St. Croix Sensory (Sensory Evaluation/Perception)

Self-promotional stickers.

DESIGN FIRM:

Eymer Design, Inc.,

Boston, Massachusetts

ART DIRECTOR/

ILLUSTRATOR:

Douglas Eymer

DESIGNER:

Selene Carlo-Eymer

PRINTING PROCESS:

1-color

Eymer Design (Graphic Design)

The logo for a house-cleaning service evokes a sense of old-fashioned American quality.

DESIGN FIRM:

Rassman Design, Denver, Colorado

DESIGNERS:

Amy Rassman, John Rassman

American Maid

DESIGN FIRM:

Wilcox Design, Atlanta, Georgia

ART DIRECTOR/

DESIGNER: Mark Wilcox

BUDGET: $2000

PRINTING PROCESS:

2-color offset

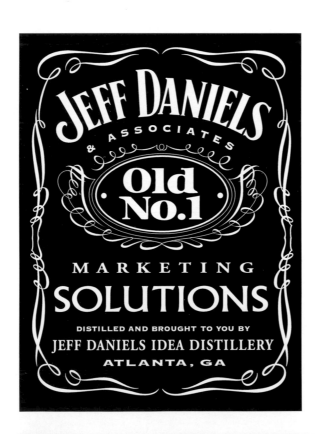

Jeff Daniels Advertising

DESIGN FIRM:

Sibley/Peteet Design,

Dallas, Texas

ART DIRECTOR:

Rex Peteet

DESIGNERS: Janet Lorch,

Rex Peteet

ILLUSTRATOR:

Janet Lorch

This corporate identity

conveys quality

craftsmanship and an Old

World feel for the product.

DESIGN FIRM:

Mires Design, San Diego,

California

ART DIRECTOR/

DESIGNER: Jose Serrano

ILLUSTRATOR:

Nancy Stahl

BUDGET: $10,000

PRINTING PROCESS:

3-color PMS

Deleo Clay Tile (Premium Clay Roofing Tile)

59

The logo identifies trails and points of interest on a section of the Minnesota bike trail system.

DESIGN FIRM:

Design Center, Minnetonka, Minnesota

ART DIRECTOR:

John Reger

DESIGNER:

Sherwin Schwartzrock

Symbol for an attorney who provides many hours of pro bono work to victims of domestic violence and others in need in her community.

DESIGN FIRM: Sina Design, Boulder, Colorado

DESIGNER: Byron Sina

BUDGET: Design: fee was waived ; printing: $500

PRINTING PROCESS: 1-color offset

Michelle E. Chess, Esq. (Attorney)

The logo establishes an identity for a research center involved in organically-inspired synthetic material systems, and is used in the center's international marketing program.

DESIGN FIRM:

Plaid River Design, Inc.,

Blacksburg, Virginia

DESIGNER:

Jennifer Goodreau

BUDGET: Design: $350 (logo); printing: $1650 (annual report), $900 (folders), $500 (mugs), $800 (T-shirts)

PRINTING PROCESS:

1- and 2-color; foil stamping

Center for Intelligent Material Systems and Structures

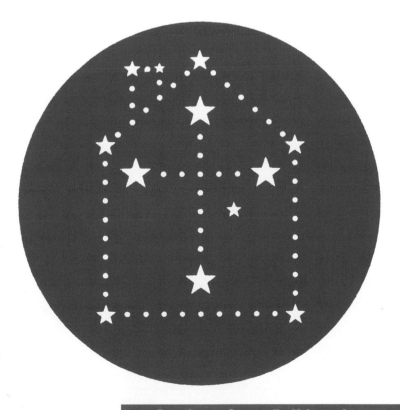

Symbol distinguishes this company from other home builders who operate along the Chesapeake Bay waterfront.

DESIGN FIRM:

Stygar Group, Inc.,

Richmond, Virginia

ART DIRECTOR/

DESIGNER:

James A. Stygar

BUDGET: $5000

PRINTING PROCESS:

2-color offset

Southern Cross Builders, Inc.

corner

bakery™

you knead it.

The logo captures the spirit of this unpretentious, friendly neighborhood bakery.

DESIGN FIRM: Adrienne Weiss Corporation, Chicago, Illinois

ART DIRECTOR/ DESIGNER/ILLUSTRATOR: Sharon Box

PRINTING PROCESS: Black and spot white tint; color logo is 4 spot PMS colors on flat ivory stock.

PAPER: Commercial Kraft paper, recyclable French Speckletone Kraft

Lettuce Entertain You, Inc./Corner Bakery

Big Fish Design (Illustration/Graphic/Industrial Design)

An identity for a small, home-based design and illustration business that also designs silkscreened T-shirts and posters for retail sale. Used in a wide variety of applications, the image reflects the humorous and whimsical nature of the majority of the firm's designs.

DESIGN FIRM: Big Fish Design, Fishers, Indiana

DESIGNER: Paul Ocepek

PRINTING PROCESS: 1-color silkscreen (T-shirt, mug); HP 650 plotter/ LaserWriter (other)

Pike Market Foundation

Logo for a capital campaign to raise public funds for superstructure maintenance (i.e., crumbling buildings) in Seattle's Pike Place Market.

DESIGN FIRM: Bill Ghoede, Seattle, Washington

ART DIRECTOR: Roy Feiring

DESIGNER/ILLUSTRATOR: Art Chantry

BUDGET: Pro bono

63

A marketing identity aimed at both retailers and consumers positions the company as blue-collar and tough.

DESIGN FIRM:

Kohnke Koeneke, Inc.,

Milwaukee, Wisconsin

ART DIRECTORS/

DESIGNERS:

Taylor Smith, Rich Kohnke

ILLUSTRATOR:

Jim McDonald

COPYWRITERS:

Denise Kohnke,

Steve Koeneke

PRINTING PROCESS:

4-color silkscreen(shirts),

2-color silkscreen (tags)

Logo for a publishing company's new division specializing in guitar-oriented recordings.

DESIGN FIRM:

Miller Freeman Publications, San Mateo, California

ART DIRECTOR/ DESIGNER: John Ueland

PRINTING PROCESS:

4-color (art/advertising); 1-color (letterhead)

A dynamic corporate image sets this yarn importer apart from its competitors in quality and scope. The logo conveys the international aspect of the company and suggests its mail-order capability, and at the same time is warm and inviting.

AGENCY:

Graves Fowler Associates, Silver Spring, Maryland

ART DIRECTOR:

Mariann Seriff

DESIGNERS:

Mariann Seriff, Jerry Dadds

ILLUSTRATOR:

Jerry Dadds

BUDGET: $1300

G O O D N E S T

Goodnest, a naturals shop concept, stands for goodness, simplicity and quality, reflected in a product line of bath and personal accessories, stationery, sheets, towels, scented candles, etc. A Goodnest line of bath and shower products was chosen to be showcased in the Smithsonian Museum as an example of eco-sensitive packaging.

AGENCY:

Adrienne Weiss Corporation, Chicago, Illinois

ART DIRECTOR/ LOGO DESIGNER:

Sharon Box

Logo for a company that provides hospitals with freelance pediatricians.

DESIGN FIRM:

Larry Smith & Associates, Atlanta, Georgia

ART DIRECTOR/ ILLUSTRATOR:

Michael Bailey

BUDGET: $1700

PRINTING PROCESS:

2-color

Pediatric Healthcare Travelers

Around the Clock

Logo for an organization that helps lower-income families obtain housing.
DESIGN FIRM:
DeLor Design Group , Louisville, Kentucky
ART DIRECTOR/
DESIGNER/ILLUSTRATOR:
Kevin Wyatt
BUDGET: Pro bono
PRINTING PROCESS:
2-color offset (brochure),
2-color silkscreen (T-shirt)

New Directions Housing, Inc.

Die Brücken Artwear

A contemporary icon for an artwear company specializing in limited-edition art graphics for T-shirts. The name "Die Brücken" refers to the German art movement Die Brücke (The Bridge) formed in the late 1800s. The logo figure is creating a bridge between the black and white sections of the design, with the bridge suggesting movement into a new area of thought.

DESIGN FIRM:
Firehouse 101 Design, Columbus, Ohio
ART DIRECTOR/
DESIGNER/ILLUSTRATOR:
Kirk Richard Smith
BUDGET: Design: $3000 (6 T-shirts + logo)
PRINTING PROCESS:
Silkscreen (T-shirts), 2-color/PMS (business cards)

Logo for a pregnancy counseling service that favors the mother keeping the child or putting it up for adoption.

DESIGN FIRM:

The Summit Group,

Irving, Texas

ART DIRECTOR/

DESIGNER/ILLUSTRATOR:

Scott Williams

BUDGET: Pro bono

The identity for this pizza and spaghetti house appears on menus, employee T-shirts, signage and other applications.

DESIGN FIRM:

Hansen Design Company,

Seattle, Washington

ART DIRECTOR:

Pat Hansen

DESIGNERS: Pat Hansen,

Kip Henrie

ILLUSTRATOR: Kip Henrie

BUDGET: Design: $2500

Sparta's Pizza and Spaghetti House

Appropriate to a multi-talented writer and editor is this image that illustrates with a double-ended pencil the concept of burning the candle at both ends.

DESIGN FIRM:

Tracy-Locke/DDB

Needham, Dallas, Texas

ART DIRECTOR/

DESIGNER/ILLUSTRATOR:

Jonathan Rice

BUDGET: $0

PRINTING PROCESS:

2-color offset

Sandra Rice (Copywriter/Book Reviewer/Editor)

This identity for a pet-care facility is used on all signage, business/appointment cards and reminder postcards.

DESIGN FIRM:

Marilyn Rose Design, Rutherford, New Jersey

ART DIRECTOR/

DESIGNER: Marilyn Rose

BUDGET: Design: $2500

PRINTING PROCESS:

1-color offset

Pet Perfect (Pet Grooming/Boarding/Supplies)

This promotional logo for the school's 50th anniversary was featured on various publications and merchandise including numerous articles of clothing.

AGENCY:

Richard Danne & Associates, New York, New York

ART DIRECTOR:

Richard Danne

DESIGNERS: Gary Skeggs (logo, stationery, press kit); Maria Kerdell, Richard Danne (clothing, bags, mugs); Richard Danne, Gayle Shimoun (LookBook); Gayle Shimoun, Richard Danne (F.I.T. Network, 50th Anniversary issue)

PRINTING PROCESS:

Multilith printing by F.I.T. Print Shop (stationery); offset, 4-color + varnish (press kit); offset, 6-color (LookBook); offset, 2-color (F.I.T. Network)

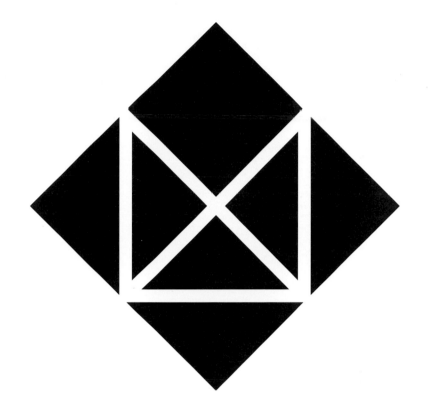

This large international construction company recently became a major steel producer. The diamond symbol with a linear *M* represents the company's traditional business activities and also embraces new ventures such as information technology.

AGENCY:

Richard Danne & Associates, New York, New York

ART DIRECTOR:

Richard Danne

DESIGNER: Gary Skeggs

PRINTING PROCESS:

Silkscreen (manual binder), offset, 3 flat colors (text pages)

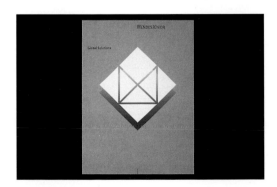

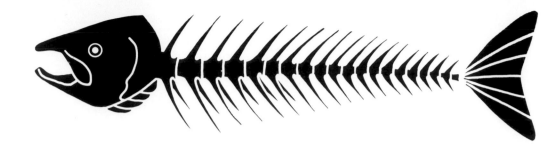

The screened back illustration on the stationery—a self-portrait of the artist as a 10-year-old fish cleaner—creates a new image for this designer/illustrator.
ART DIRECTOR/
DESIGNER/ILLUSTRATOR:
Karen Williamson, Seattle, Washington
BUDGET: Design: $0; printing: $2000 (total package)
PRINTING PROCESS: 2-color, offset with % screen

Logo depicts the country setting of this community of single-family homes.
DESIGN FIRM: Lehner & Whyte, Inc., Montclair, New Jersey
ART DIRECTORS/
DESIGNERS: Hugh Whyte, Donna Lehner
ILLUSTRATOR: Hugh Whyte
BUDGET: Design: $3500; printing: $1500

Corporate identity for a firm specializing in fashion photography, marketing, and advertising.

DESIGN FIRM:

Kathleen Burgund Design, Atlanta, Georgia

DESIGNER:

Kathie Burgund

ILLUSTRATOR:

Elizabeth Traynor

BUDGET: $1400

Michael Belk & Company

The owner's nickname, Cave Dog, provided the name and corporate identity for his multimedia production company.

DESIGN FIRM:

Powell Design Office, Dallas, Texas

ART DIRECTOR:

Glyn Powell

DESIGNER/ILLUSTRATOR:

Jon Buell

PRINTING PROCESS:

1-color, offset

Cave Dog Productions (Audio/Video Multimedia Production)

This freelance designer/ computer artist prints her basic logo on a laser printer. Rubber stamps provide variations on the basic design—in winter, the light produces snow; in spring, flowers and bees, etc.

DESIGNER/ILLUSTRATOR: Katherine A. Flynn, Ridgefield, Connecticut

BUDGET: Printing: less than $750

PRINTING PROCESS: Laser printer, rubber stamping

Osborn and DeLong (Graphic Design)

DESIGN FIRM: Osborn and DeLong, Bloomington, Illinois

ART DIRECTOR/ DESIGNER: Al Fleener

BUDGET: Design: $1800

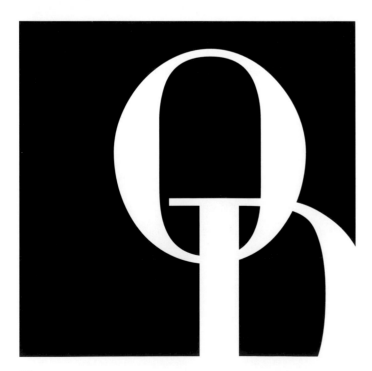

Logo for a clothing line for a local surf shop reflects the funky beach culture of Southern California.

DESIGN FIRM:

Mires Design, San Diego, California

ART DIRECTOR/

DESIGNER: Scott Mires

ILLUSTRATOR:

Gerald Bustamante

BUDGET: $8500

PRINTING PROCESS:

2-color, silkscreened on garments

Full Bore Surf Shop

For his company logo, Pujol sought a simple graphic element with a touch of humor and personal meaning. He chose the rooster, an ancient symbol of France, his native country.

DESIGN FIRM:

Henry Pujol Design Group, Philadelphia, Pennsylvania

ART DIRECTOR/

DESIGNER/ILLUSTRATOR:

Henry Pujol

BUDGET: Design: $750; printing: $750

PRINTING PROCESS:

2 PMS colors, offset lithography

Henry Pujol Design Group

This tri-part identity represents the diversity of the store's clientele and the wide variety of eyeglasses available. The three icons appear on three versions of the store's business card to fit the personality of the moment.

DESIGN FIRM:
Zeewy Design, Paoi, Pennsylvania

ART DIRECTOR:
Orly Zeewy

DESIGNERS: Lia Calhoun, Orly Zeewy

BUDGET: Design: $4000; printing: $1750 for 18,000 cards (1000 @ 18 lots)

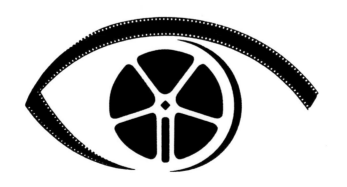

INDIANA FILM SOCIETY

Identity for a group that recognizes and awards work by film and video makers who live in or hail from Indiana.

AGENCY:
Young & Laramore, Indianapolis, Indiana

ART DIRECTOR:
Jeff Laramore

ILLUSTRATORS:
Scott Montgomery, Jeff Laramore

Indiana Film Society

Promotional logo for the Council's seminar on opportunities in marketing the arts.

DESIGN FIRM: Firehouse 101 Design, Columbus, Ohio

DESIGNER/ILLUSTRATOR. Kirk Richard Smith

PRINTER: Century Graphics

BUDGET: Design: $1200

PRINTING PROCESS: 2 flat PMS colors; illustration technique was cut amberlith

Greater Columbus Arts Council

These symbols were developed to support and identify the contents of a newsletter: focus report (top left), questions and answers (top right), business issues (bottom left), physician profile (bottom right).

AGENCY: IDEART, Inc., Fort Collins, Colorado

DESIGNER: Susan Bacheller-Stewart

BUDGET: $750

Poudre Valley Hospital

The symbol has a
traditional financial and
investment feel, but with
a contemporary look.

DESIGN FIRM:

Design Center,

Minnetonka, Minnesota

ART DIRECTOR:

John Reger

DESIGNER:

Sherwin Schwartzrock

Schumacher Investment Group (Financial Planning)

DESIGN FIRM:

Sibley/Peteet Design,

Dallas, Texas

ART DIRECTOR:

Rex Peteet

DESIGNER/ILLUSTRATOR:

Diana McKnight

Lullaby (Baby Clothes/Linens Retail Store)

Computerized network for tracking lost pets.

DESIGN FIRM:

Sam Smidt, Inc., Palo Alto, California

ART DIRECTOR/

DESIGNER: Sam Smidt

PRINTING PROCESS:

Offset

ANIMAL TRACKING NETWORK

PetNet

The company image, a flying horse, is a simplified rendering of a wing and a horse.

DESIGN FIRM:

S&S Design Studio, Hillsborough, New Jersey

ART DIRECTOR:

Sunny Sang

DESIGNER:

T-H (Dennis) Sun

BUDGET: Pro bono

Chi-Am Tours (Tours for Chinese Groups)

INTERNATIONAL WINE & BEER FESTIVAL

ON THE POTOMAC

International Wine & Beer Festival on the Potomac

Saturday, October 23, 1993
Harbour Park in Georgetown
Wisconsin Avenue & K Streets, N.W.
11:00 am to 6:00 pm

• A benefit for Bread for the City and Zacchaeus Free Clinic
• Free wine or beer glass
• International music, food, dancing

For ticket information, call
703-764-2399
Sponsored by the
Wine Tasting Association

$12 in advance, $15 at the gate • $5 under 21 and non-drinkers • Children under 12 free

Promotion for a benefit sponsored by the Wine Tasting Association to raise funds for this free clinic/food distribution center in Washington, DC.
DESIGN FIRM:
Levine and Associates, Washington, DC
ART DIRECTOR/
DESIGNER:
J. Michael Myers
PRINTER: DeLancey Printing, Alexandria, Virginia
BUDGET: Design: $500 (20% of regular fee); printing: donated (poster)
PRINTING PROCESS:
3-color (poster)

Zacchaeus Free Clinic

Promotional symbol for the sound-design capabilities of this video and film post-production house.
DESIGN FIRM:
Gibbs Baronet, Dallas, Texas
ART DIRECTORS:
Willie Baronet, Steve Gibbs
DESIGNERS:
Kellye Kimball, Willie Baronet
BUDGET: Design: $1000; printing: $800
PRINTING PROCESS:
1-color, offset

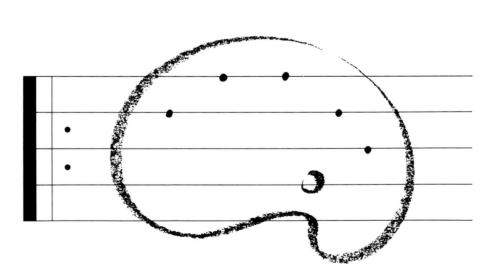

West End Post

Musician's promotional logo appears on cassettes, business cards, stationery, etc.
ART DIRECTOR:
Karen Williamson, Seattle, Washington

Anabel (Musician)

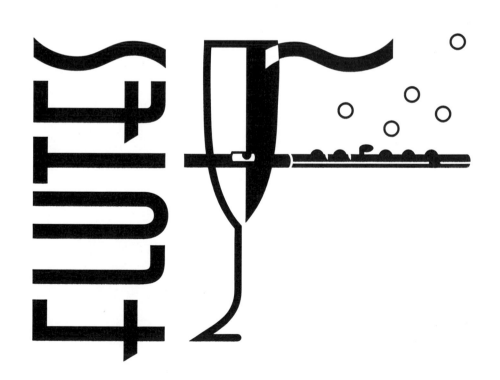

Flutes Jazz Club/Restaurant

Logo promotes the club's dual attraction with its depiction of the musical instrument and the champagne glass.
DESIGN FIRM:
Bennett Peji Design, San Diego, California
ART DIRECTOR:
Bennett Peji
DESIGNER/ILLUSTRATOR:
Chakra Kusuma
BUDGET: $5000
PRINTING PROCESS:
2 match colors

Corporate identity for developers and producers of educational consumer multimedia products.
DESIGN FIRM: Zida Borcich Letterpress, Fort Bragg, California
ART DIRECTOR/ DESIGNER: Zida Borcich
ILLUSTRATOR: Michael McMillan (flying TV set)
BUDGET: Design: $2000; production: $2000
PRINTING PROCESS: All letterpress printed on Heidelberg Windmill using hand-set lead type and ornaments.

Paradesa Media

This educational, residential and vocational center for children and adults suffering mental retardation needed an identity to initiate fundraising efforts. A direct-mail piece followed—then a benefit performance by jazz musician Dave Brubeck.
DESIGN FIRM: EAT Design, Kansas City, Missouri
ART DIRECTOR/ DESIGNER/ILLUSTRATOR: Patrice Eilts-Jobe
BUDGET: $1500 partially pro bono
PRINTING PROCESS: 3 PMS, 4-color process

LAKEMARY
CENTER

Lakemary Center

This identity for an interior designer/space planner can be used for both commercial and residential markets.

DESIGN FIRM:

Dave Lafleur Design, Denver, Colorado

ART DIRECTOR/

DESIGNER: Dave Lafleur

ILLUSTRATOR:

Chris McKay

BUDGET: Design: $850;

printing: $350

PRINTING PROCESS:

2-color, offset

Sitescapes (Landscape Architecture)

DESIGN FIRM:

California Design International, San Francisco, California

ART DIRECTOR:

Linda S. Kelley

DESIGNER/ILLUSTRATOR:

Dan Liew

BUDGET: $1500

PRINTING PROCESS:

4-color, sheet-fed

Logo for a charitable organization that supports and aids students in the besieged Bosnian capital.

DESIGN FIRM:

Salpeter Design, Inc., New York, New York

ART DIRECTOR/ DESIGNER/ILLUSTRATOR:

Bob Salpeter

BUDGET: Pro bono

PRINTING PROCESS:

2 color, offset

Saving Sarajevo's Students

DESIGN FIRM:

Mark Oldach Design, Chicago, Illinois

ART DIRECTOR:

Mark Oldach

DESIGNER: Mark Meyer

BUDGET: Design: barter for writing services; printing: $1200

PRINTING PROCESS:

2-color, offset

"m^r!ene:m@rks."

Marlene Marks (Writer/Marketing Consultant)

DESIGN FIRM:

Kilmer, Kilmer & James, Inc.,

Albuquerque, New Mexico

ART DIRECTORS/

DESIGNERS:

Brenda Kilmer, Richard

Kilmer

Griffin & Associates (Business Consulting)

This logo for the heavy
metal band Morbid
Sacrifice is edgy and
counter-culture, yet
projects a serious
professionalism.

DESIGN FIRM:

Richard Leeds Design,

San Mateo, California

ART DIRECTOR/

DESIGNER: Richard Leeds

BUDGET: Design: $250

PRINTING PROCESS:

Main applications are

photocopying and 2-color

T-shirt silkscreening

Morbid Sacrifice

**100% ALL
NATURAL
COMPUTER
FREE ART**

This identifying mark was applied to all packaging and illustration tissues as well as final art to indicate that the art was produced the old-fashioned way.

DESIGN FIRM:
Chickinelli Studios,
Omaha, Nebraska
ART DIRECTOR:
Mark Chickinelli

DESIGNERS: Ron Saack,
Mark Chickinelli
ILLUSTRATORS:
Mark Chickinelli, Ryle Smith
BUDGET: $250
PRINTING PROCESS:
Rubber stamp, 2-color labels

Mark Chickinelli (Illustration)

A manufacturer of historical wooden miniatures wanted a quality image that could be reproduced easily and on an extremely low budget.

DESIGN FIRM:
Art Kirsch Graphic Design,
Palo Alto, California
ART DIRECTOR:
Art Kirsch

DESIGNER/ILLUSTRATOR:
Char Kirsch
BUDGET: Design: pro bono; printing: supplied by a friend—client paid for buyouts
PRINTING PROCESS:
1-color, offset

Reminiscence

"Camel design" is a term used to describe bad advertising.

ART DIRECTOR:
Kurt Steinwand, Safety Harbor, Florida

PRINTER: Promocom Printing, Pinellas Park, Florida

BUDGET: Printing: donated

PRINTING PROCESS:
3-color, traditional printing

This logo re-introduced Kubin-Nicholson as a printer of *all* large-format applications, not just billboards.

AGENCY:
Young & Laramore, Indianapolis, Indiana

CREATIVE DIRECTORS:
David Young, Jeff Laramore

ART DIRECTOR:
Carolyn Hadlock

ILLUSTRATORS:
David Wariner, Scott Montgomery

COPYWRITER:
Charlie Hopper

BUDGET: Design: $7300; printing: $62,000 (stationery, envelopes, notecards, etc.)

PRINTING PROCESS:
2 hits of white (stationery, first run), 2 hits of white, dry trapped (stationery, second run), 4 additional PMS colors

Kubin-Nicholson

DESIGN FIRM:

Sibley/Peteet Design,

Dallas, Texas

ART DIRECTOR/

DESIGNER: David Beck

ILLUSTRATORS:

David Beck, Mike

Broshous

Charles James (Personal Fitness Trainer)

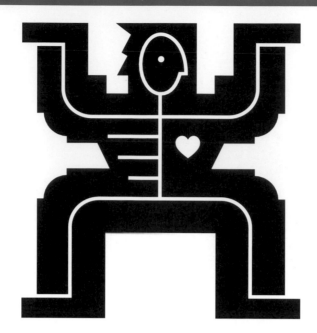

A limited budget meant that much of the design/production work for this identity program was done by hand (pre-made tags, photocopying).

DESIGN FIRM:

Richard Fire Design,

Los Angeles, California

ART DIRECTOR:

David Jervis

DESIGNERS: Richard Fire,

David Jervis

BUDGET: Design: $100

approximately; printing:

$200 (excluding T-shirts)

PRINTING PROCESS:

Photocopy and silkscreen

"Man must evolve for all human conflict a method which rejects revenge, aggression and retaliation. The foundation of such a method is love."

MARTIN LUTHER KING, JR.

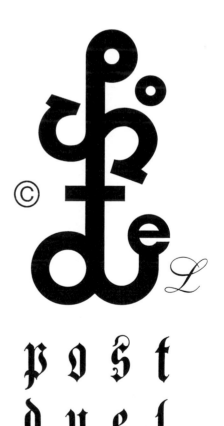

Post Duel (Retail/Wholesale/Mail Order Clothing)

Olympic Graphics (Printer)

The symbol calls attention to the precision and quality of work produced by this shop.

DESIGN FIRM: Design Center, Minnetonka, Minnesota

ART DIRECTOR: John Reger

DESIGNERS: Kobe, Todd Spichke

PRINTING PROCESS: Posters were printed in 4-color to introduce the new symbol.

Parachute (Graphic Design)

Parachute is the design facility of Clarity Coverdale Fury Advertising. The parachute image is meant to symbolize the firm's ability to skillfully and comfortably navigate its customers through the battle-zone of marketing communications.

DESIGN FIRM: Parachute, Minneapolis, Minnesota

ART DIRECTOR/ DESIGNER: Bob Upton

PRINTING PROCESS: 3-color offset

Texas Association for Retarded Citizens (ARC)

DESIGN FIRM:

Gavos & Helms, Dallas,

Texas

ART DIRECTOR:

David Helms

DESIGNER/ILLUSTRATOR:

Amy Stephenson

BUDGET: Pro bono

North Texas Women's Soccer Association

DESIGN FIRM:

Sibley/Peteet Design,

Dallas, Texas

ART DIRECTOR/

DESIGNER:

Donna Aldridge

PRINTING PROCESS:

Silkscreen

Glaxo Inc. (Pharmaceuticals)

Identity for Glaxo's Child Health Recognition award program in which clients provide funds for grass-roots organizations that, in turn, support and promote the health of children.

DESIGN FIRM:

BlackBird Creative, Raleigh, North Carolina

ART DIRECTOR:

Holly Russell/Glaxo Inc.

DESIGNER/ILLUSTRATOR:

Patrick Short

BUDGET: Design: $1700

PRINTING PROCESS:

Primarily offset

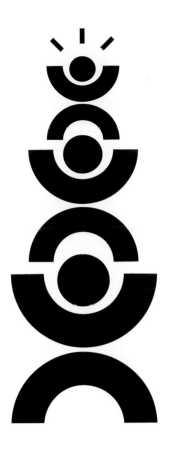

Paul N. Kalish, D.D.S./Alison C. Stapakis, D.D.S.

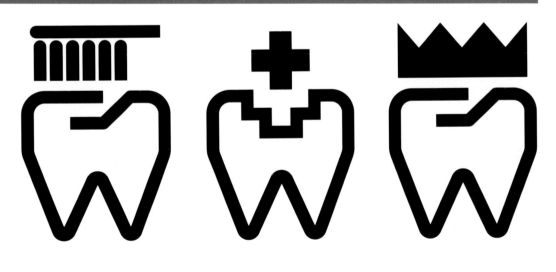

Identity for a dental practice specializing in general, implant and cosmetic dentistry.

DESIGN FIRM:

Ervin Montague Design, Long Beach, California

ART DIRECTORS:

Lori Ervin, Darrell Montague

DESIGNER: Lori Ervin

ILLUSTRATOR:

Darrel Montague

BUDGET: Design: $3000 (logo/identity system); printing: $3500

PRINTING PROCESS:

2-color (PMS gray + special match purple), offset

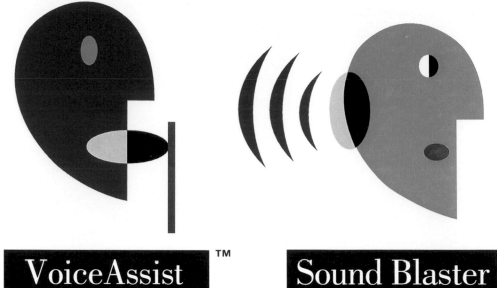

Each logo depicts an individual product and indicates compatibility with the other products.

DESIGN FIRM:
Cahan & Associates,
San Francisco, California
ART DIRECTOR: Bill Cahan
DESIGNER: Sharrie Brooks

VoiceAssist™

Sound Blaster™

Video Blaster™

ShareVision™

Creative Labs (Multimedia Products)

Logo depicts plastic surgery as an art form, not just a medical procedure. The tropical colors evoke the locale of the practice—Miami.
DESIGN FIRM:
Borchew Design Group, Inc., Deerfield, Illinois
ART DIRECTOR:
Michael Borchew
DESIGNER:
Jackie Borchew
BUDGET: Design: $5000; printing: $5000
PRINTING PROCESS:
2-color, offset

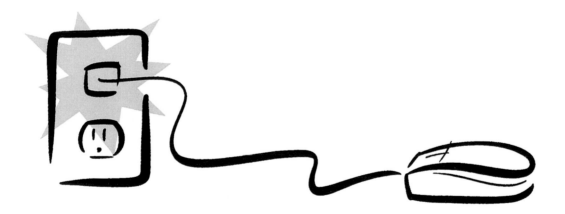

Symbol for PowerTalk, a series of workshops run by this developer of client/server, application development, and data analysis tools.
DESIGN FIRM: Group 121, Boston, Massachusetts
CREATIVE DIRECTOR:
Robert Davis
ART DIRECTOR:
Ellen Weinberger
ILLUSTRATOR:
Sandra Bruce
BUDGET: Design: $26,000 (design development for initial brochure, which included logo)
PRINTING PROCESS:
2-color, offset

Logo depicts the style and friendly atmosphere of this upscale, trendy New York City restaurant.

DESIGN FIRM:

John Kneapler Design, New York, New York

ART DIRECTOR/

DESIGNER: John Kneapler

ILLUSTRATORS:

John Kneapler, Matt Waldman

PRINTING PROCESS:

Hot stamped on recycled paper

Zoë (Restaurant)

Image uses the connection between human and animal features to signify human/animal co-existence.

DESIGN FIRM:

Peterson & Company, Dallas, Texas

ART DIRECTOR/

DESIGNER: Scott Ray

ILLUSTRATOR:

Mary Lynn Blassuta

BUDGET: Logo was part of Society's annual report budget

Dallas Zoological Society

CARR DESIGN

Playing off the company name, this logo for a new design firm boosts public/client awareness of the company. Costs were substantially reduced by printing the letterhead on various colors of paper, and then imprinting various business forms on a laser printer.

DESIGN FIRM: Carr Design, Bountiful, Utah

DESIGNER: Dave Titensor

BUDGET: Design: $900; printing: $1400 (for all components)

PRINTING PROCESS: 3 spot colors, offset

Identity for an Italian bistro located in the hotel.

DESIGN FIRM: Associates Design, Northbrook, Illinois

CREATIVE DIRECTOR: Chuck Polonsky

DESIGNER: Beth Finn

BUDGET: Design: $1500

PRINTING PROCESS: 3 spot colors (menu with inserts)

Symbol for a federal agency established to advise businesses on how to comply with the Americans with Disabilities Act.
DESIGN FIRM: Design Works, Wichita Falls, Texas
ART DIRECTOR/ DESIGNER: Steve St. John
BUDGET: $800

Federal Compliance Corporation

Abstractions of the first letters of the principals' last names communicate the nature of the firm's work.
DESIGN FIRM: Cloud and Gehshan Associates, Inc., Philadelphia, Pennsylvania
ART DIRECTOR: Jerome Cloud
DESIGNERS: Jerome Cloud, Bradford Kear
BUDGET: Printing/ diecutting: $16,000
PRINTING PROCESS: Engraving, offset lithography, die-cutting

Cloud and Gehshan Associates, Inc. (Environmental Design)

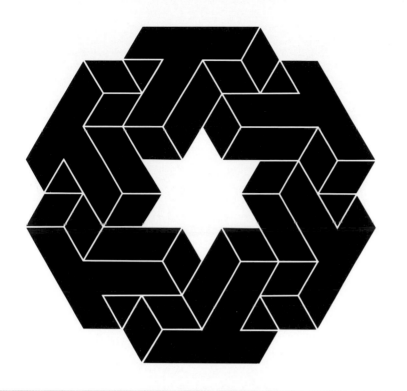

Symbol for a travel agency specializing in tours to Israel and the Middle East.
DESIGN FIRM:
Pentagram Design,
New York, New York
ART DIRECTOR/
ILLUSTRATOR:
Michael Gericke

North Star Travel

The theme of National Condom Week—"Safe sex. Safe love."—was symbolized by two condoms that form a negative heart between them, indicating that condoms protect true love from AIDS.
DESIGN FIRM:
S&S Design Studio,
Hillsborough, New Jersey
ART DIRECTOR:
Sunny Sang
DESIGNER:
T-H (Dennis) Sun
BUDGET: Pro bono

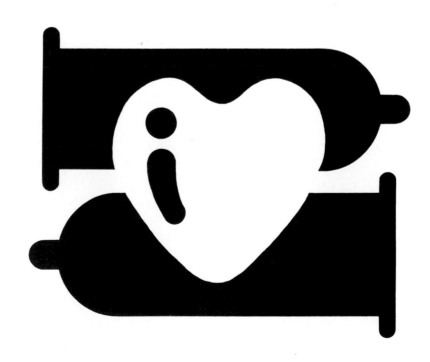

National Condom Week (AIDS Benefit)

Skein Domain

Promotional logo for a new yarn/knitting store.

DESIGN FIRM:

Mañana Design, Burlington, Vermont

ART DIRECTOR/

DESIGNER/ILLUSTRATOR:

Anthony Sini

BUDGET: Design: $1000;

printing: $200 (cards)

PRINTING PROCESS:

1 PMS

Doradel Pictures (Independent Filmmakers)

The lizard motif, inspired by Native American art, is an apt identity for the principals, who are from the Southwest. The logo also acts as a talisman: the lizard is a survivor in a tough environment, just as an independent film company needs to be a survivor in the tough environment of Hollywood.

DESIGN FIRM:

Cats Pajamas, Inc., St. Paul, Minnesota

ART DIRECTOR:

Mike Hazard

DESIGNER/ILLUSTRATOR:

Patricia Olson

BUDGET: Design: $4000;

printing: $1250

PRINTING PROCESS:

2 spot colors, offset lithography

Municipalities are the primary market for this leader in video production, and form a pivotal part of the logo design.

DESIGN FIRM:
Shawver Associates, Pleasanton, California

ART DIRECTOR:
Mark Shawver

DESIGNER/ILLUSTRATOR:
Brian Kuehn

BUDGET: In trade

PRINTING PROCESS:
2-color, offset

This identifying logo is applied, via rubber stamp, to all the department's property. The dog is configured using *P* and *D* letters from the Futura and Futura Extra Bold font. T-shirts sporting the design were produced for employees.

DESIGN FIRM:
Hallmark Cards, Kansas City, Missouri

ART DIRECTOR/
DESIGNER: James Caputo

BUDGET: Cost effective—minimal

PRINTING PROCESS:
Canon Copy heat transfer (T-shirt)

Hat in the Cat

...MEOWSA!

A zany visual for a wardrobe stylist for the film and TV industries. Originally, each element of the client's stationery was to have a different hat on the cat's stomach—but the allusion to Dr. Seuss's hat was so successful that it alone was used.

AGENCY: Luzzi Limited, New York, New York
ART DIRECTOR/
DESIGNER/ILLUSTRATOR: Jay Sylvester
BUDGET: Design/production were donated as a wedding gift and the client handled the printing.
PRINTING PROCESS: 2-color, thermography

Capons Rotisserie Chicken

The logo focuses on the rotisserie style of cooking as this restaurant chain's motif. The chicken's body becoming a spinning tornado is meant to suggest the chain's quick take-out service.
DESIGN FIRM:
Hornall Anderson Design Works, Seattle, Washington
ART DIRECTOR:
Jack Anderson

DESIGNERS: David Bates, Jack Anderson
ILLUSTRATORS:
David Bates, George Tanagi

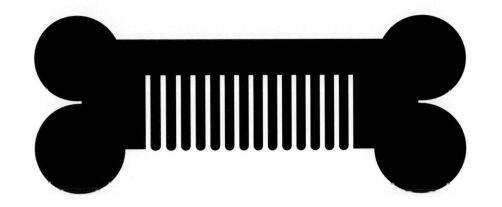

DESIGN FIRM:

Sibley/Peteet Design,

Dallas, Texas

ART DIRECTOR/

DESIGNER: Derek Welch

Bow Wow Barber (Dog Groomer)

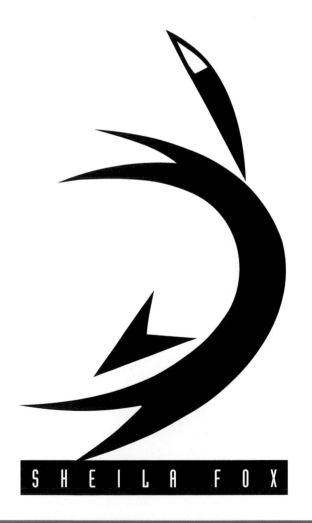

S H E I L A   F O X

This whimsical promotional

logo plays on the client's

last name as a visual cue to

her personality.

DESIGN FIRM:

Henderson Tyner Art Co.,

Winston-Salem, North

Carolina

ART DIRECTOR/

DESIGNER: Troy Tyner

BUDGET: Under $1000

PRINTING PROCESS:

2-color, offset

Sheila Fox (Broadcast Production)

101

MEYERS
CLEANING
SERVICE

Adobe Illustrator was
used to distort the type
in this logo.
DESIGN FIRM:
Jager Associates, Grand
Rapids, Michigan
ART DIRECTOR: Lee Jager
DESIGNER: Gayle Raymer
PHOTOGRAPHER:
Steve Milanowski
BUDGET: $3500
PRINTING PROCESS:
2-color

Meyers Cleaning Service (Industrial/Residential Cleaning)

Commemorative logo for
the fifth anniversary of a
free-standing out-patient
surgery center.
DESIGN FIRM:
Engel + Tirak, Erie,
Pennsylvania
ART DIRECTOR/
DESIGNER:
Karen S. Johnson,
Cleveland, Ohio
ILLUSTRATOR: Pete Smith
BUDGET: Design: $600
(T-shirt); production:
$1125 (250 T-shirts)
PRINTING PROCESS:
Black-and-white,
silkscreen

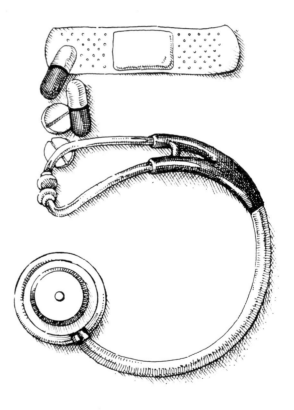

St. Vincent Surgery Center

Tropical identity for the hotel's pool bar.

DESIGN FIRM:

Associates Design, Northbrook, Illinois

CREATIVE DIRECTOR:

Chuck Polonsky

DESIGNER: Jill Arena

BUDGET: Design: $1000

PRINTING PROCESS:

4-color (menu and check presenter)

Big Hand Productions (Compact Disk Interactive/Computer Animation)

This identity moves and interacts with the viewer when used on-screen—the logo character walks, dances, and even rides a horse.

DESIGN FIRM:

Cindy Slayton Creative, Irving, Texas

CREATIVE DIRECTOR:

Cindy Slayton

ART DIRECTOR/

DESIGNER/ILLUSTRATOR:

Robin Cox Schippel

BUDGET: Design: $3000 tradeout; printing: $2000

PRINTING PROCESS:

1-color

B I G

H A N D

103

Identity for a magazine-
sponsored awards show
honoring technological
breakthroughs in
computer networking.
DESIGN FIRM:
Eymer Design, Inc.,
Boston, Massachusetts
ART DIRECTOR/
DESIGNER:
Douglas Eymer
BUDGET: $8000
PRINTING PROCESS:
2-color

Network World (Computer Industry Publication)

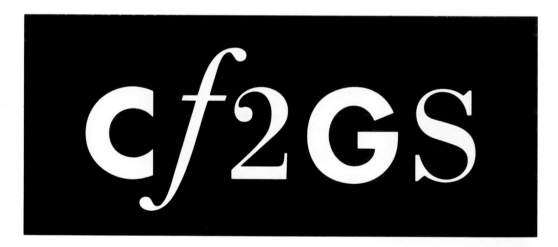

An acronym of the five
partners' names—
Christiansen, Fritsch,
Giersdorf, Grant and
Sperry—projects a unified
corporate image while
retaining their individual
personalities.
DESIGN FIRM:
Hornall Anderson Design
Works, Seattle,
Washington
ART DIRECTOR:
Jack Anderson
DESIGNERS: David Bates,
Jack Anderson

CF2GS (Marketing Communications Firm)

A simple, smiling face made from the number 49 identifies the station with entertainment and lends it a youthful image to match its demographics. Animated on-air with a simple wink of the eye, during the Saturday kids' shows, the logo is defaced with a colorful mustache and funny hair.

DESIGN FIRM:
Sandstrom Design, Portland, Oregon
DESIGNER: George Vogt
BUDGET: Design: $7500
PRINTING PROCESS:
2 PMS + black, offset

Identity for an advertising agency's cross-country ski team.
DESIGN FIRM:
Fallon McElligott, Minneapolis, Minnesota
ART DIRECTOR/
DESIGNER: Joe Paprocki
BUDGET: $250
PRINTING PROCESS:
Silkscreen

Promotional identities for two sports-themed fundraisers—Golf Fall 1994 and Basketball Spring 1994.
AGENCY:
Carmichael Lynch, Minneapolis, Minnesota
DESIGN FIRM:
Way Cool Creative, St. Paul, Minnesota
ART DIRECTOR/
DESIGNER: Peter Winecke
ILLUSTRATORS:
Mark Herman (golf), Peter Winecke (basketball)

Seattle American Diabetes Association

Promotional identity for Winter 1994 hockey tournament.
AGENCY:
Carmichael Lynch, Minneapolis, Minnesota
ART DIRECTOR/
DESIGNER/ILLUSTRATOR:
Peter Winecke

West End Hockey (Youth Hockey)

106

H

HARMONY
collection

The objective was to devise a logo for a blended cotton knit fabric collection. An adaptation of two bass clef symbols creates the *H*, and the music staff refers not only to musical harmony, but also to the blending of the cotton knit fibers.

DESIGN FIRM:
Parham Santana Inc.,
New York, New York
ART DIRECTOR/
DESIGNER: Millie Hsi

Identity for a musical series featuring world-class chamber music in unusual architectural settings within the Seattle area.
DESIGN FIRM:
Hornall Anderson Design Works, Seattle , Washington
ART DIRECTOR: Jack Anderson
DESIGNERS: David Bates, Jack Anderson, Julia LaPine
ILLUSTRATOR:
David Bates

This logo is for a non-profit, inner-city, self-help organization conceived and formulated by the Carter Center in Atlanta. It communicates the hope and possibilities that can occur when neighbors join hands to help one another and themselves.
DESIGN FIRM:
Wages Design, Atlanta, Georgia
ART DIRECTOR/
DESIGNER/ILLUSTRATOR:
Ted Fabella

THE ATLANTA PROJECT

The Atlanta Project

Promotional logo for an annual community gathering and music festival promoting inter-denominational and interracial cooperation.
DESIGN FIRM:
Joseph Rattan Design, Plano, Texas
ART DIRECTOR/
DESIGNER: Joe Rattan

Lovers Lane United Methodist Church

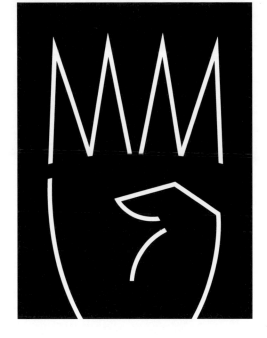

Commemorative logo for Meltzer & Martin's fourth anniversary.

DESIGN FIRM:

Sullivan Perkins, Dallas, Texas

ART DIRECTORS:

Ron Sullivan, Dan Richards

DESIGNER: Dan Richards

PRINTING PROCESS:

2-color, silkscreen

Hallowfest

A FAMILY FESTIVAL BENEFITING THE CENTER FOR PUPPETRY ARTS

Center for Puppetry Arts

Promotional logo for the fall fundraising festival of this non-profit museum and theater.

DESIGN FIRM:

Young & Martin Design, Atlanta, Georgia

ART DIRECTOR/

DESIGNER/ILLUSTRATOR:

Ed Young

BUDGET: Pro bono

PRINTING PROCESS:

2 Day-Glo inks + black

Symbol for a pianist, vocal coach, singer, and story-teller who does all of these things simultaneously.

DESIGN FIRM:

Dogstar Design and

Illustration, Birmingham,

Alabama

ART DIRECTOR/

DESIGNER/ILLUSTRATOR:

Rodney Davidson

BUDGET: In trade for vocal coaching and piano accompaniment.

DESIGN FIRM:

Dogstar Design and

Illustration, Birmingham,

Alabama

ART DIRECTOR/

DESIGNER/ILLUSTRATOR:

Rodney Davidson

BUDGET: In trade for piano repair and a lifetime of tunings.

Kirk Alford (Piano Tuning/Voicing/Repair)

Designed for the head of the voice department at a local university, this logo promotes private voice lessons offered to students from outside the university. Middaugh is apparently the type of teacher who really does take students under his wing.

DESIGN FIRM:

Dogstar Design and Illustration, Birmingham, Alabama

ART DIRECTOR/ DESIGNER/ILLUSTRATOR:

Rodney Davidson

BUDGET: In trade for voice lessons

PRINTING PROCESS:

1-color on laser printer

Promotional logo for a private vocal studio.

DESIGN FIRM:

Dogstar Design and Illustration, Birmingham, Alabama

ART DIRECTOR/ DESIGNER/ILLUSTRATOR:

Rodney Davidson

BUDGET: In trade for vocal coaching

PRINTING PROCESS:

Laser printer

111

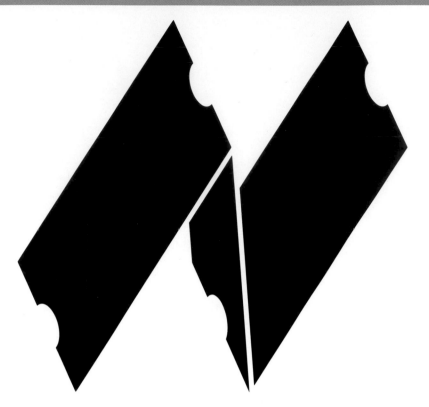

This easily recalled icon immediatly identifies the firm as a dispenser of tickets to sundry entertainments via electronic terminals requiring a credit card. The logo was needed for potential national use. DESIGN FIRM: Visual Partners, Inc., New York, New York ART DIRECTOR: Kathryn Manzo Morris DESIGNER: Frank Morris BUDGET: Design: based on use—$2500 (local), $5000 (regional); $10,000 (national)

Communication Institute

Promotional logo for the Marketing and Communications Department at the University of Utah. DESIGN FIRM: DCE Graphic Design, Salt Lake City, Utah ART DIRECTOR: Scott Greer DESIGNER/ILLUSTRATOR: Cody Rasmussen

Go Group (International Entertainment/Design Network)

GO GROUP
ENTERTAINMENT AND
DESIGN NETWORK

LOUIS C. ALLEN

27 LAFAYETTE STREET
SARATOGA SPRINGS
NEW YORK 12866, USA
TEL/FAX: 518•581•8123

DESIGN FIRM: Idee Design,

South Glens Falls, New York

ART DIRECTOR/

DESIGNER:

Marjolaine Arsenault

BUDGET: Design: $1500

PRINTING PROCESS:

1-color + blind embossing

(business card)

DESIGN FIRM:

Europa Design, Atlanta,

Georgia

ART DIRECTOR/

DESIGNER:

Françoise Heckhausen

BUDGET: $2500

PRINTING PROCESS:

2 PMS + black

Europa Design, Inc. (Graphic Design)

Gift certificate logo reflects the upscale quality of this fashion retailer.
DESIGN FIRM: Nordstrom Advertising,
Portland, Oregon
ART DIRECTOR: Cheryl Zahniser
DESIGNER: Alison Grevstad
CALLIGRAPHER: Anton Kimball
PRINTING PROCESS: 2 PMS + a gold foil, offset

Nordstrom Advertising

The logo for this health spa's initial venture into the retail food business conveys a feeling of quality, earthiness, and freshness.
DESIGN FIRM: Tana & Co., New York, New York
ART DIRECTOR/ DESIGNER: Tana Kamine
ILLUSTRATOR: Anthony Russo
BUDGET: Design: $125,000 (logo/identity program); printing: $125,000 (includes all pieces of the program)
PRINTING PROCESS: Various; packaging was 3- and 4-color offset

Canyon Ranch Spa Cusine

Text and image contained within a circle creates a bull's-eye effect for this logo that helps consumers locate the product amid others on the shelf. The logo also has an appealing farm-fresh feel.

DESIGN FIRM:

The Marlin Company, Springfield, Missouri

CREATIVE DIRECTOR:

Michael Stelzer

ART DIRECTOR/

DESIGNER/ILLUSTRATOR:

Matt Graif

PRINT PRODUCTION:

Bill Mamorella

BUDGET: Design: $4000 (logo/stationery); $18,000 (packaging)

PRINTING PROCESS:

2 flat inks + metallic bronze (stationery); flexo + metallic bronze (packaging)

The logo elegantly communicates the tradition of Italian espresso for a chain of minibars.

DESIGN FIRM:

Milani Design, New York, New York

ART DIRECTOR/

DESIGNER:

Armando Milani

BUDGET: Design: $20,000; printing: $15,000

PRINTING PROCESS:

1-color (brown) + gold embossing (cup only)

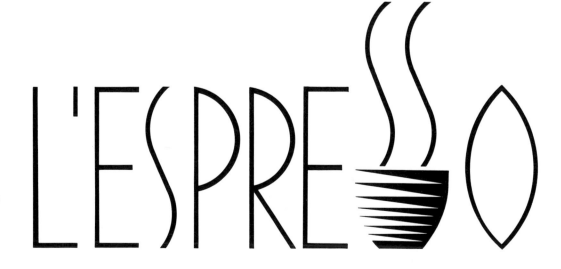

L'Espresso

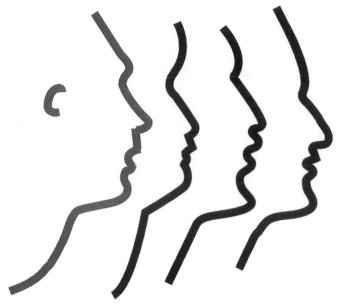

Designed to promote awareness of Dr. Gall's surgical practice in a highly competitive market, the logo conveys an impression of proficiency and caring for a diverse patient base.

DESIGN FIRM:

John Milligan Design, Largo, Florida

ART DIRECTOR/ ILLUSTRATOR:

John Milligan

DESIGNER:

Michael Milligan

BUDGET: Design/ production: $7500

PRINTING PROCESS:

4-color

Alan M.Gall M.D.
Ear·Nose·Throat·Head·Neck Surgery

Alan M. Gall, M.D. (Otolaryngology)

The image for this counseling center illustrates the idea that growth (leaves) can come from personal trauma (broken heart).

DESIGN FIRM:

Bonnie Liefer Graphic Design, Pittsburgh, Pennsylvania

ART DIRECTOR/ DESIGNER: Bonnie Liefer

BUDGET: Design: $500; printing: $1132

PRINTING PROCESS:

2 PMS + black

Center for Pastoral Psychology

A simple name and bold image communicate the professional, high-quality, friendly service provided by this audiologist/hearing aid manufacturer/retailer.

DESIGN FIRM:
The Puckett Group,
Atlanta, Georgia

ART DIRECTOR:
Kent Puckett
DESIGNER: Matt Smartt
BUDGET: $10,000–
$15,000
PRINTING PROCESS:
3-color, offset

Pacific Design Center (Furniture Showplace/Design Mart)

DESIGN FIRM:
Pentagram Design,
San Francisco, California
ART DIRECTOR:
Kit Hinrichs
DESIGNER: Mark Selfe

117

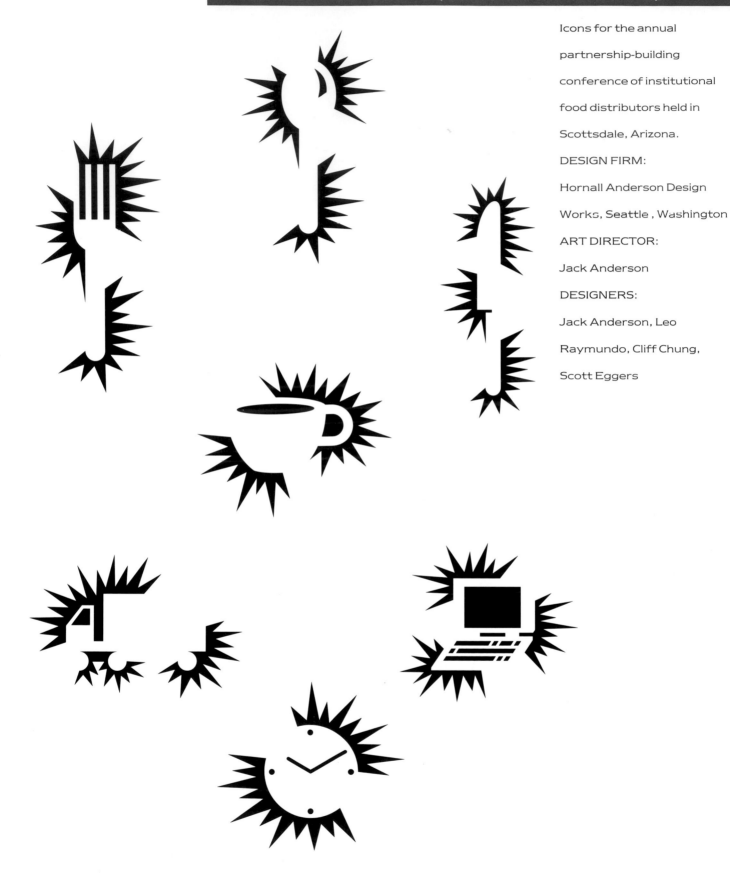

Icons for the annual partnership-building conference of institutional food distributors held in Scottsdale, Arizona.

DESIGN FIRM:

Hornall Anderson Design Works, Seattle , Washington

ART DIRECTOR:

Jack Anderson

DESIGNERS:

Jack Anderson, Leo Raymundo, Cliff Chung, Scott Eggers

A series of state-sanctioned logos developed for Iowa's tourism division are licensed to vendors of approved goods (such as wearables) for a fee. The logos are also used to promote community activities, festivals and events.

DESIGN FIRM:
Sayles Graphic Design,
Des Moines, Iowa
ART DIRECTOR/
DESIGNER: John Sayles

State of Iowa

The firm's name is
reinforced by requiring
the reader to actually
pivot the logo in order to
read it in all formats
ranging from business
cards to a flipbook
moving announcement.
DESIGN FIRM:
Pivot Design, Chicago,
Illinois
ART DIRECTOR/
DESIGNER:
Brock Haldeman
PRINTING PROCESS:
2-color, lithography

Pivot Design, Inc.

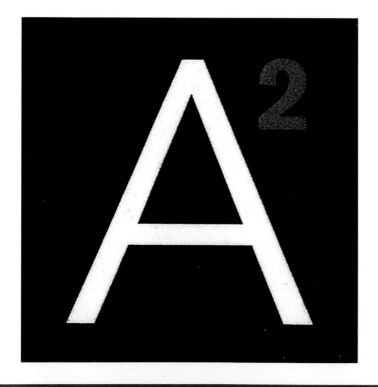

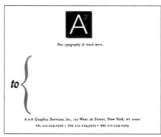

The A² logo for this pre-
press, production, output
house represents the
father and son owners,
Allan and Adam.
DESIGN FIRM:
Adam Greiss Design,
New York, New York
ART DIRECTOR/
DESIGNER: Adam Greiss
TYPOGRAPHY/
PRODUCTION:
Adam Wahler

A to A Graphic Services, Inc.

The corporate identity for Nordstrom Factory Direct, a retailing venture of Nordstrom, is based on the acronym NFD. The *N* and *D* are sans-serif letters that convey a 25%-off warehouse look. The scripted *F* in the middle bespeaks designer-quality fashion. The resulting message is that NFD offers designer-quality fashion in a warehouse environment.

DESIGN FIRM:

Hornall Anderson Design

Works, Seattle, Washington

ART DIRECTOR:

Jack Anderson

DESIGNERS:

Jack Anderson, Cliff Chung,

David Bates

The letterforms in this logo reflect mathematical symbols used in computer programming.

AGENCY:

Advent Design Agency, Inc., Elkhart, Indiana

DESIGNER:

Ronald A. Schemenauer

BUDGET: Design: $600; printing: $655 (envelope, business card, letterhead)

PRINTING PROCESS:

3-color, offset (envelope, business card, letterhead)

Xeno (Computer Systems Consulting & Analysis)

B!BS
BETTER INFANT BEGINNINGS

Identity for a health insurance company's prenatal care program for expectant mothers.
DESIGN FIRM: Langton Cherubino Group, Ltd., New York, New York
ART DIRECTORS: Norman Cherubino, David Langton
ILLUSTRATOR: Ted Stern
BUDGET: Design: $14,500 (logo/marketing materials); printing: $32,000 (marketing materials)
PRINTING PROCESS: 4-color, offset

Home Life Financial Assurance Corporation

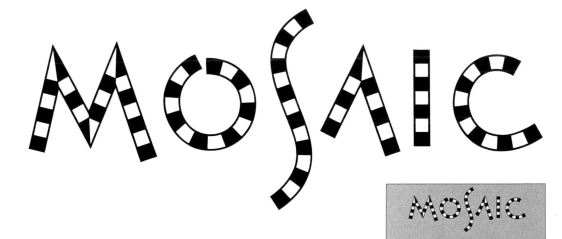

The idea for the Mosaic letterforms came first, in turn providing the name for this jewelry business.
DESIGN FIRM: Opal Arts, Chicago, Illinois
DESIGNER: Scott Wampler
BUDGET: Design: $500; printing: $350
PRINTING PROCESS: 2-color, offset

Mosaic

Logo for a change-of-
address card.
DESIGNERS: John Bowers,
Helene Jonson,
Ann Arbor, Michigan

John Bowers/Helene Jonson (Graphic Design)

DESIGN FIRM:
Muller & Company,
Kansas City, Missouri
DESIGNER: David Shultz

Chris Muller (Software)

A photographer's distinctive face, widely recognized in the region, provided the perfect identity when he started his own studio.

DESIGN FIRM:

Graphic Design Continuum, Dayton, Ohio

ART DIRECTOR/

DESIGNER:

Dwayne Swormstedt

PHOTOGRAPHER:

Bill Swartz

BUDGET: Design: in trade for photographic services

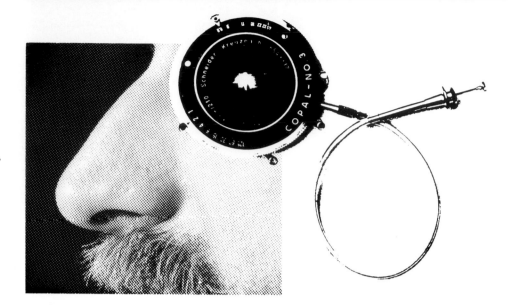

A commercial studio photographer's identity reflects her wit and creativity, as well as her photographic style.

DESIGN FIRM:

Next Year's News, Toledo, Ohio

ART DIRECTOR/

DESIGNER: Paula D. Ashley

BUDGET: Design: $450 (billed at 1/2 rate); printing: $350

PRINTING PROCESS:

1-color, offset + die-cut Rolodex card

Shoot For The Moon Photography Studio

Identity deftly
communicates the
character of this film and
video production studio.
DESIGN FIRM:
Walsh & Associates,
Seattle, Washington
ART DIRECTOR/
DESIGNER:
Michael Stearns
BUDGET: Design: $5200;
printing: $625
PRINTING PROCESS:
Black ink on laid stock;
white foil stamp + deboss
square (business card)

BROWNE
PRODUCTION GROUP
————
Eric Browne
3429 Airport Way S.
Seattle, WA 98134
206 . 382 . 0591

Browne Productions

An in-house corporate
photographer, Kinch
bought the studio from the
parent company. The logo
describes the nature of the
business to potential new
clients while informing
existing clients of the
change of ownership and
the new approach to
corporate photography.
DESIGN FIRM:
Communication by Design,
Portland, Oregon

DESIGNER:
Richard M. Anderson
BUDGET: Design: $1500;
printing: $800
PRINTING PROCESS:
Offset + thermography
(business card), offset
(letterhead)

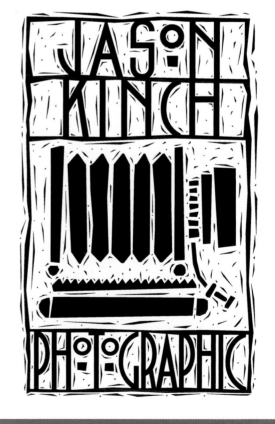

Jason Kinch Photographic

The logo stresses the human aspects of the field of internal corporate communications consulting.

DESIGN FIRM:
The Weller Institute for the Cure of Design, Park City, Utah

ART DIRECTORS:
Don Weller, Kevin Sheehan/Praxis
DESIGNERS: Don Weller, Chikako Weller
ILLUSTRATOR: Don Weller
BUDGET: Design: $3000 (logo), $1000 (application)
PRINTING PROCESS: 2-color, offset

P R A X I S

Praxis

The two faces represent the College of Education and Psychology's focus on interaction—between faculty and student, faculty and faculty, students and students, and alumni and the children and adults they will eventually serve.

DESIGN FIRM:
Seran Design, Harrisonburg, Virginia
ART DIRECTOR/
DESIGNER: Sang Yoon
BUDGET: $200
PRINTING PROCESS: 2-color

James Madison University

A promotional symbol positions this hair stylist/makeup artist as someone who works with younger and more venturesome customers. It was printed on a business card that was trimmed and inserted into die-cut slits in a moving announcement.

DESIGN FIRM: Minnick Advertising and Design, Louisville, Kentucky
ART DIRECTOR/ DESIGNER: Norman L. Minnick
BUDGET: Design: $800 (logo); under $1500 for entire package (logo/card/announcements)
PRINTING PROCESS: 3-color, offset

Elizabeth Moore

A personable, friendly dentist uses a logo to communicate her warmth and sense of humor to the people in her community. The logo appears on business stationery, an informational brochure and other direct mail pieces.

DESIGN FIRM: Energy Energy Design, Campbell, California
ART DIRECTOR/ DESIGNER/ILLUSTRATOR: Leslie Guidice
PRINTING PROCESS: 2-color

SUSAN CALIRI

D.D.S.

Susan Caliri, D.D.S.

Restroom signs for a

graphic design office.

DESIGN FIRM:

Wood Design,

New York, New York

ART DIRECTOR/

DESIGNER: Tom Wood

ILLUSTRATOR:

Mayda Freije

PRINTING PROCESS:

Etched in metal

Wood Design

Logo for a promotional

T-shirt.

ART DIRECTOR:

Alice Drueding

DESIGNER/ILLUSTRATOR:

Lance Rusoff, Doylestown,

Pennsylvania

Club Genesis

128

Logo for a store selling

natural bodycare products.

DESIGN FIRM:

Tharp Did It!, Los Gatos,

California

CREATIVE DIRECTOR:

Diane Richardson

ART DIRECTOR:

Cerstin Cheatham

DESIGNERS: Rick Tharp,

Gail Hall

ILLUSTRATORS:

Susan Jaekel, Rick Tharp

PRINTING PROCESS:

2-color, offset on Kraft

label stock

Body Chemistry

Promotional logo for a

Christian organization that

works with disadvantaged

youth.

DESIGN FIRM:

John Evans Design,

Dallas, Texas

ART DIRECTOR/

DESIGNER/ILLUSTRATOR:

John Evans

BUDGET: Pro bono

Rainbow Bridge

Symbol shows the variety
of printing processes
available to this printing
broker.

DESIGN FIRM:

Kevin Akers, Designer,

San Rafael, California

ART DIRECTOR/

DESIGNER/ILLUSTRATOR:

Kevin Akers

BUDGET: $6000

PRINTING PROCESS:

4-color, offset + embossing

Marcia Skinner/Ink Well

Project Survival

Promotional logo for the
primary fundraiser for a
public-service youth project
that combines educational
programs and basketball.

DESIGN FIRM:

Morgan State University,

Baltimore, Maryland

ART DIRECTOR/

DESIGNER/ILLUSTRATOR:

Joseph Ford

BUDGET: Design: donated;

printing: $500

PRINTING PROCESS:

2-color, offset

Finally there's a better way our
Stockton kids can spend free time

The logo for this non-profit,
church-run activity center
incorporates a certain
street appeal to reach the
kids most in need of this
type of positive outlet.
Fundraising/promotional
materials featuring
the logo are mailed to
area business leaders.
DESIGN FIRM:
Graphica, Inc.,
Miamisburg, Ohio
ART DIRECTOR/
DESIGNER: Greg Simmons
BUDGET: Design: $2500;
printing: $2500
PRINTING PROCESS:
2-color

FreeZone (Sports Activity Center)

Logo for a fiery copywriter
with an extraordinary
mane of red hair.
DESIGN FIRM:
Mintz + Hoke Design,
Avon, Connecticut
DESIGNER/ILLUSTRATOR:
Wayne Raicik
BUDGET: Design: $500;
printing: $1000
PRINTING PROCESS:
3 PMS

JANET UNGER
redwriter

Janet Unger (Copywriter)

Promotional logo for a store-sponsored Mother's Day event held at the zoo for kids and their moms.

DESIGN FIRM:

Ken Shafer Design, Seattle, Washington

ART DIRECTOR/ DESIGNER/ILLUSTRATOR:

Ken Shafer

PRINTING PROCESS:

Silkscreen

DESIGN FIRM:

Tom Fowler, Inc., Stamford, Connecticut

ART DIRECTOR:

Elizabeth P. Ball

DESIGNER/ILLUSTRATOR:

Samuel Toh

Bull's Head Animal Hospital

Logo for a song publishing division of Atlantic Records specializing in independent bands.
DESIGN FIRM:
Eat the Worm Graphics, Staten Island, New York
ART DIRECTOR/
DESIGNER/ILLUSTRATOR:
Bruce Erik Brauer
BUDGET: Design: $500; printing costs absorbed by Atlantic Records
PRINTING PROCESS:
4-color

Dog Society Songs Publishing Co.

The puppy illustration identifies this firm as a children's video production company.
DESIGN FIRM:
Lisa Levin Design, Mill Valley, California
ART DIRECTOR: Lisa Levin
DESIGNERS: Lisa Levin, Jill Jacobson
ILLUSTRATOR:
Michael Schwab

Firedog Pictures

Commemorative logo for
Hornall Anderson Design
Work's 10th anniversary.
DESIGN FIRM:
Hornall Anderson Design
Works, Seattle,
Washington
ART DIRECTOR:
Jack Anderson
DESIGNERS:
Jack Anderson, David
Bates, Lian Ng
ILLUSTRATOR:
Yutaka Sasaki

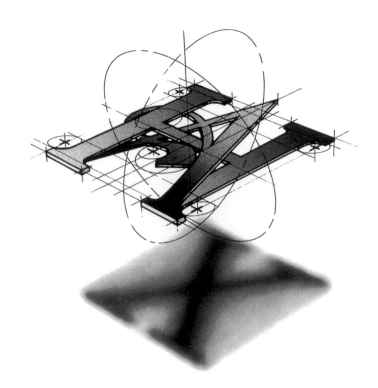

Hornall Anderson Design Works (Graphic Design)

Logo for a coalition that
supports a moratorium on
further building on the
national mall in
Washington, DC.
DESIGNER: John Bowers,
Ann Arbor, Michigan
BUDGET: Pro bono

no More Monuments on the Mall

Coalition to Preserve the Mall

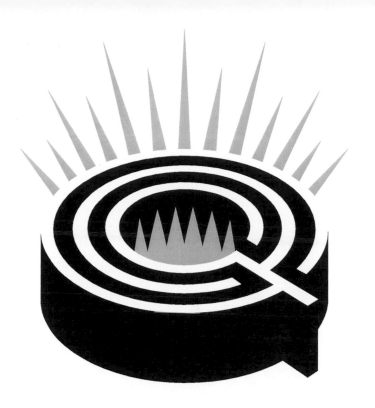

The identity for this marketing, advertising and design company depicts the guidance offered to primarily sports-related clients in sorting through a maze of ideas to find the most rewarding solution.

DESIGN FIRM: Q4L Marketing, Inc., Richmond, Virginia

ART DIRECTOR: Jack Kauffman

DESIGNER: Judy Rumble

BUDGET: Printing: $2500

PRINTING PROCESS: 2-color (stationery), 2-color + varnish (business cards), 1-color + yellow foil stamp (mechanical and computer disk labels)

Q4L Marketing, Inc.

The logo for this employee-owned wood shutter manufacturer instantly conveys the concept of shutters and associates that idea with the company name. It appears on trucks, building, T-shirts, etc. The logo needed to work in 1-color.

DESIGN FIRM: After Hours, Phoenix, Arizona

ART DIRECTOR/ DESIGNER: Russ Haan

BUDGET: $1500

PRINTING PROCESS: 1-color, offset lithography

Cover-ups in high places.

If decorating hard-to-reach areas has you troubled, consider top-quality wooden shutters. Every shutter is hand crafted by our employee-owners. And since we've already worked with dozens of your neighbors, you know we're reliable. Call for your free buyer's guide. And instigate a cover-up the public will admire.

Weaver Quality Shutters
218 South 15th Street Phoenix, Arizona 85034 (602)267-7000

Weaver Quality Shutters

135

DESIGN FIRM:

Brainchild Design Team,

Columbia, Missouri

ART DIRECTOR/

DESIGNER: Steve Hicks

ILLUSTRATOR:

Michelle Hicks

BUDGET: Design: $500

PRINTING PROCESS:

4-color, silkscreen

The logo was designed to
represent a series of
stories throughout the
newspaper about the
growing business
opportunities in the new
Russia.

DESIGN FIRM:

The Columbus Dispatch,

Columbus, Ohio

ART DIRECTOR/

DESIGNER: Scott Minister

136

Signature logo for a summer event series—music/comedy/dance—held in a historic area of Denver.

DESIGN FIRM:

Weber Design, Inc., Denver, Colorado

DESIGNER: Martin Gregg

BUDGET: Design: pro bono

PRINTING PROCESS:

4-color, silkscreen banners

Larimer Square

Kekuilani Development Company (Residential Builder)

Identity for a plantation style housing community built on the site of an old pineapple and sugar cane plantation. Although the designers preferred this solution, the client chose another design for the final logo.

DESIGN FIRM:

Martin Stevers Design, Encinitas, California

ART DIRECTOR/

DESIGNER/ILLUSTRATOR:

Martin Stevers

BUDGET: Design: $3000

PRINTING PROCESS:

4-color

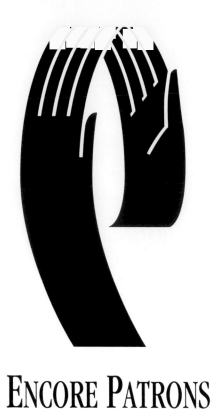

ENCORE PATRONS

(ăn´kôr, ăn kôr´)
int. again!
n. song, etc. added
by demand;
n. a demand for
reappearance made
by an audience;
an additional
performance in
response to such a
demand.

Identifying icon for a
special patrons' group
among the supporters of
the Dallas Symphony.
DESIGN FIRM:
Tom Lout and Company,
Dallas, Texas
ART DIRECTOR/
DESIGNER: Tom Lout
BUDGET: Pro bono
PRINTING PROCESS:
4-color

Dallas Symphony

Basic symbol for an overall
corporate identity that will
be easily and inexpensively
reproducible on various
start-up materials.
DESIGNER:
Joan Stevenson,
Takoma Park, Maryland

Phyllis Colomabaro Family Dentistry

Symbol for a new identity

program.

DESIGN FIRM:

Smit Ghormley Lofgreen,

Phoenix, Arizona

ART DIRECTOR:

Brad Ghormley

DESIGNERS:

Brad Ghormley, Steve

Smit, Art Lofgreen, Doug

Dearden

BUDGET: $5000

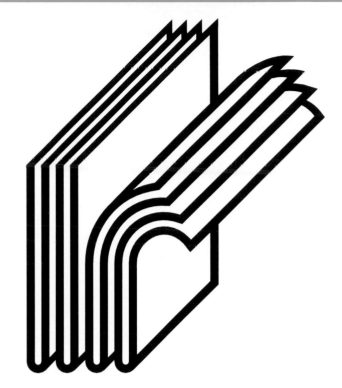

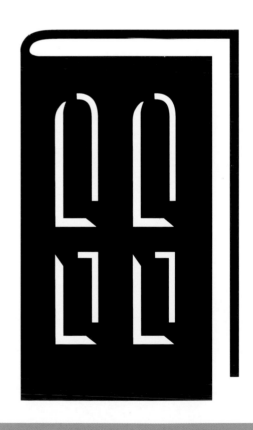

Promotional logo for an

upscale custom home

builder.

DESIGN FIRM:

Greg Welsh Design,

Seattle, Washington

ART DIRECTOR/

DESIGNER/ILLUSTRATOR:

Greg Welsh

BUDGET: Design: $1500

First Edition Homes

Promotional logo for a new aquarium/hands-on learning center.

DESIGN FIRM:

Dogstar Design and Illustration, Birmingham, Alabama

DESIGNER/ILLUSTRATOR:

Rodney Davidson

CREATIVE DIRECTOR:

George Fuller

The Sea Science Center

Pacific IBM Employees Federal Credit Union

Logo for CURES, a confidential, 24-hour mortgage information service. The name is an acronym for CU Real Estate Services, a wholly-owned subsidiary of the credit union.

DESIGN FIRM:

Hull & Honeycutt, Sacramento, California

ART DIRECTOR/

DESIGNER: Susan Hull

ILLUSTRATOR:

Annette Mirviss

BUDGET: $2000

Alan Ross (Landscape & Environmental Photography)

Identity package reflects this landscape/ environmental photographer's classic methods of working and suggests an emphasis on outdoor subject matter.

DESIGNER:

Michael Schwab, Santa Fe, New Mexico

LETTERPRESS:

Julie Holcomb

BUDGET: Design: $4800; printing: $2000

PRINTING PROCESS:

Black-and-white, letterpress

Promotional identity for the Unity Through Diversity annual ceremony and dinner honoring achievement in the areas of education, leadership and community service.

DESIGN FIRM:

Hinshaw, Young & Partners, Oakland, California

DESIGNER/ILLUSTRATOR:

Carrie English

BUDGET: Design: $800

PRINTING PROCESS:

Silkscreen (banner)

Career Resources Develpment Center (CRDC)

Visual identity for Windows on the World Restaurant, created as part of the New York Restaurant Group's bid to manage the restaurant at the top of the New York World Trade Center. The contract to run the restaurant ultimately went to another management group.

DESIGN FIRM:
Marilyn Rose Design, Rutherford, New Jersey
ART DIRECTOR/ DESIGNER/ILLUSTRATOR:
Marilyn Rose

BUDGET: Design: $3500 (for presentation only)
PRINTING PROCESS: Color output from Fiery and IRIS

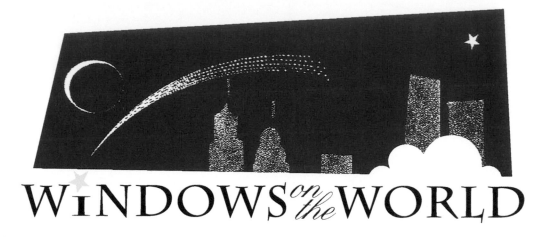

New York Restaurant Group

DESIGN FIRM:

The Pushpin Group,

New York, New York

ART DIRECTOR:

Seymour Chwast

DESIGNER:

William Bevington

PRINTING PROCESS:

4-color

Arch Associates (Quilt Importers)

142

The logo for this freelance advertising copywriter acts as a seal of quality for her writing projects. Designed as a rubber stamp, the logo adds low-cost color and versatility to her self-promotion campaign.

DESIGN FIRM:

Adele Bass & Co. Design, Pasadena, California

ART DIRECTOR/

DESIGNER/ILLUSTRATOR:

Adele Bass

BUDGET: Design: $1200;

printing: $500

PRINTING PROCESS:

1-color offset + rubber

stamp

Sharynn Bass

Symbol for a two-bottle liqueur box illustrates the slogan "Chase it with something cold." The penguin—a beer—is chasing a devil—Red Hot Schnapps—with the devil's own pitchfork.

AGENCY: Beeline Group

DESIGN FIRM:

Tharp Did It!, Los Gatos, California

DESIGNERS: Rick Tharp, Jean Mogannam

ILLUSTRATORS:

Rick Tharp (silhouette),

John Mattos (airbrush)

PRINTING PROCESS:

4-color offset

Hiram Walker (Liqueurs)

Promotional symbol for the 1992 Spring sales meeting signals this leading-edge cable company's new direction.

DESIGN FIRM:

Salvo Design Group, Newport Beach, California

ART DIRECTOR/

DESIGNER/ILLUSTRATOR:

Anthony Salvo

BUDGET: Design: $1500

PRINTING PROCESS:

4 PMS colors, offset

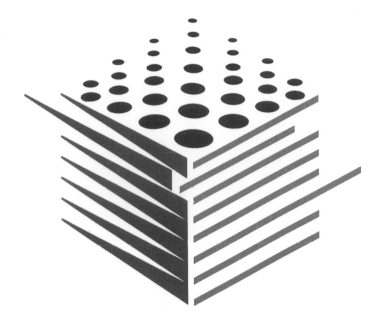

Dimension Cable

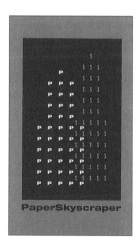

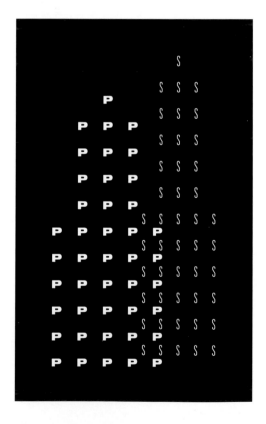

DESIGN FIRM:

Brinkley Design, Charlotte, North Carolina

DESIGNER: Leigh Brinkley

ILLUSTRATOR:

Irma de Jong

PRINTING PROCESS:

2-color

Paper Skyscraper (Bookstore/Gift Shop)

144

IDEAS AND SOLUTIONS

Corporate identity for a firm providing marketing and utility auditing services.

DESIGN FIRM:

Lambert Design Studio, Dallas, Texas

ART DIRECTOR:

Christie Lambert

DESIGNER/ILLUSTRATOR:

Joy Cathey

BUDGET: $5000

PRINTING PROCESS:

2-color, offset

Black & Hayes

Corporate identity for a firm that publishes books on hotel architecture and design, as well as work- and family-related issues.

DESIGN FIRM:

SHR Perceptual Management, Scottsdale, Arizona

ART DIRECTOR/

DESIGNER/ILLUSTRATOR:

Douglas Reeder

BUDGET: $7500

PRINTING PROCESS:

3-color (2 PMS + black)

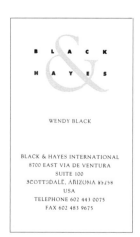

WENDY BLACK

BLACK & HAYES INTERNATIONAL
8700 EAST VIA DE VENTURA
SUITE 100
SCOTTSDALE, ARIZONA 85258
USA
TELEPHONE 602 443 0075
FAX 602 483 9675

South Coast Consulting

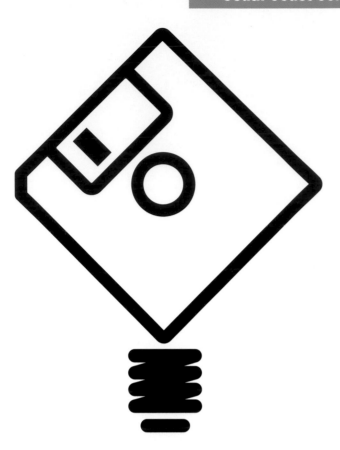

Corporate symbol depicts the bright ideas of problem-solving computer programmers.

DESIGN FIRM: Graphics Network, Long Beach, California

ART DIRECTOR/ ILLUSTRATOR: Tom Cutter

DESIGNER: Mike Scanlan

BUDGET: Design: $1000; printing: under $300

PRINTING PROCESS: 2-color, offset

David Mathis (Electrical Engineer)

Using the form of an electric plug as his first initial, this electrical engineer breaks away from conventional imagery to convey a personality a bit beyond the ordinary.

DESIGN FIRM: Raul Varela Graphic Design, Dallas, Texas

ART DIRECTOR/ DESIGNER: Raul Varela

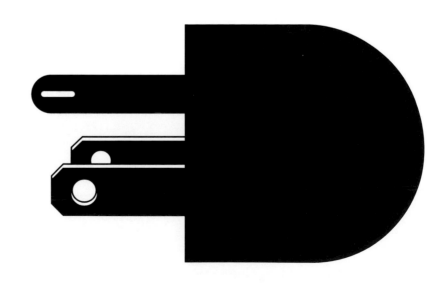

Cellular Users Billing System/CUBS

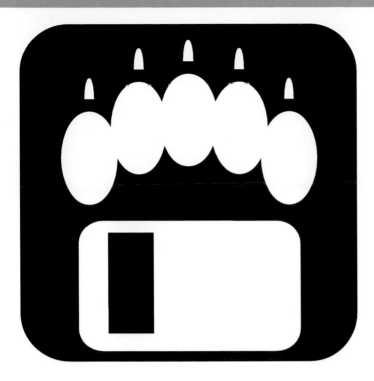

This symbol quickly identifies CUBS as a software program targeted to a specific audience—cellular phone companies.

DESIGN FIRM:
Designsense/McCabe & Duvall, Portland, Maine
DESIGNER: Dan Howard
BUDGET: Design: $5500 (includes copywriting); printing: $4500
PRINTING PROCESS: 2- and 3-color, offset

Hilltop Computing (Software)

DESIGN FIRM:

Walker Design,

Albuquerque, New Mexico

DESIGNER/ILLUSTRATOR:

Dori Gordon Walker

BUDGET: Design: $400;

printing: $150

PRINTING PROCESS:

1-color, offset

Logos were designed for every project/product released by this small, independent record company. The TV set was for a record by Astro-Man. ART DIRECTOR/ DESIGNER: Art Chantry, Seattle, Washington BUDGET: $0

Estrus Records/Dave Crider

Identity for a partnership of entertainment and music companies that includes an independent record label, a recording studio, and a film/video publisher. All separations were created with photo CD and, although there was some difficulty in color accuracy, this new technology sharply cut production fees.

DESIGN FIRM:
Imagemarc Design Studio, Fair Lawn, New Jersey
ART DIRECTOR/
ILLUSTRATOR:
Marc Passarelli
BUDGET: Design: $12,000; printing: $4800
PRINTING PROCESS:
4-color, offset; 2-color silkscreen (CD surface)

WFB Productions

Promotional logo for a CD release.

AGENCY: KMK Design, Chicago, Illinois

DESIGNER:

Karen M. Koziatek

BUDGET: Design: $900 (includes rights)

PRINTING PROCESS:

4-color (on CD), 1-color

Introductory logo for a TV show targeting teenage viewers. The logo was used in all print promotion as well as in the animation for the opening lead-in and trailer.

DESIGN FIRM:

Modern Dog, Seattle, Washington

ART DIRECTORS:

Scott St. John, Michael Strassburger

DESIGNER:

Michael Strassburger

Fox Television

150

1994 PHILADELPHIA
AIDS WALK
FROM ALL WALKS OF LIFE

This was the winning entry in a contest, sponsored by AIGA/ Phildelphia, for students at Tyler School of Art to design an identity for the 1994 AIDS Walk. The winner was chosen by the board of directors of the AIDS Walk organization, a community volunteer group founded in 1987 to raise funds for AIDS education, prevention, and services.

ART DIRECTORS:

Alice Drueding, Nicholas Rook

DESIGNER/ILLUSTRATOR:

Lance Rusoff, Doylestown, Pennsylvania

BUDGET: pro bono

Promotional logo for a fundraising event—a one-mile run for children in kindergarten through 8th grade—to benefit the hospital's pediatric therapy program. The proceeds help provide treatments for children without insurance or whose insurance or government aid has expired.

DESIGN FIRM:

Graphic Edition, Inc., Terre Haute, Indiana

ART DIRECTOR:

Brian Miller

DESIGNER/ILLUSTRATOR:

John Molloy

BUDGET: Design: $750; printing: in-house

Union Hospital

Promotional logo for a
retirement community
providing a total-care
package—health,
entertainment and basic
needs.
DESIGN FIRM:
Dogstar Design and
Illustration, Birmingham,
Alabama
ART DIRECTOR/
DESIGNER/ILLUSTRATOR:
Rodney Davidson

Woodland Village Retirement Community

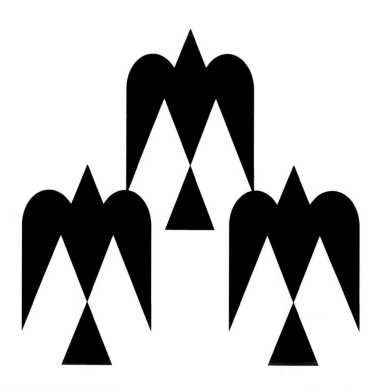

Kansas Health Foundation Leadership Institution

Promotional logo for a
philanthropic health
organization.
DESIGN FIRM:
Gardner + Greteman,
Wichita, Kansas
ART DIRECTORS/
DESIGNERS: Bill Gardner,
Sonia Greteman
BUDGET: $3000
PRINTING PROCESS:
2-color

Symbol used in an ad in support of American Way magazine's sales rep team in the National League Softball Championship program.

DESIGN FIRM:

American Way Magazine, Ft. Worth, Texas

ART DIRECTOR/

DESIGNER/ILLUSTRATOR:

Kyle Dreier

BUDGET: $0

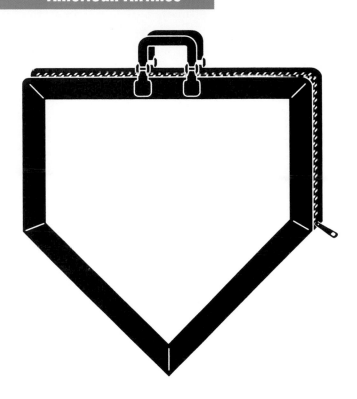

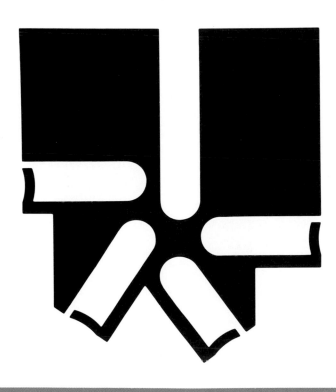

Promotional logo for a professional organization representing professors and instructors at the university.

DESIGN FIRM:

James Peters Design, Inc., Honolulu, Hawaii

ART DIRECTOR:

Allen Pollock/Loomis & Pollock Advertising

DESIGNER/ILLUSTRATOR:

James Peters

BUDGET: $1000

Promotional logo for a
filmmaking business.
Complete promotional
package included video
labels and stationery, as
well as T-shirts and caps.
DESIGN FIRM:
Jon Flaming Design,
Dallas, Texas
ART DIRECTOR/
DESIGNER: Jon Flaming
BUDGET: Design: $3500;
printing: $3500
PRINTING PROCESS:
2 PMS colors + black foil
stamp, offset

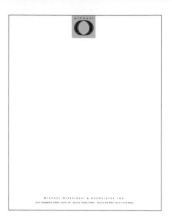

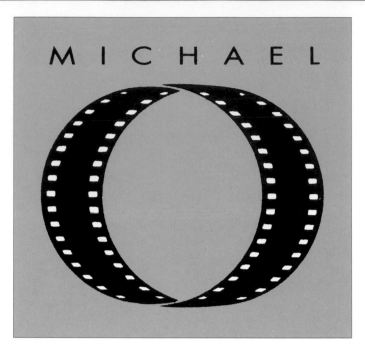

DESIGN FIRM:
Ron Kellum, Inc.,
New York, New York
DESIGNERS: Ron Kellum,
Beverly McClain

Eye to Eye Creative Solutions (Advertising)

DESIGN FIRM:

Tim Smith Design

Communications, Dublin,

Ohio

ART DIRECTOR/

DESIGNER: Tim Smith

HTIMS

Tim Smith Design Communications (Graphic Design)

Department headings in
Microsoft's corporate
newsletter.

DESIGN FIRM:

Ken Shafer Design,

Seattle, Washington

ART DIRECTOR/

DESIGNER: Ken Shafer

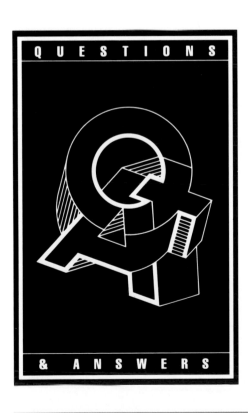

QUESTIONS

& ANSWERS

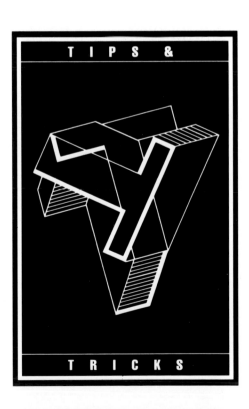

TIPS &

TRICKS

Microsoft (Computer Software)

Identifying logo for the food court of a newly renovated shopping center in Canoga Park, California. Chowzer characters were also developed to identify male, female and family restrooms

DESIGN FIRM: Sullivan Perkins, Dallas, Texas

ART DIRECTOR/ DESIGNER: Art Garcia

PRINTING PROCESS: Mediums included offset printing, silkscreen and three-dimensional fabrication

CenterMark Properties/Topanga Plaza

Promotional logo for an orthopedic center.

DESIGN FIRM: Pictogram Studio, Washington, DC

ART DIRECTOR: Hien Nguyen

DESIGNERS: Hien Nguyen, Stephanie Hooton

BUDGET: Design: $2500

Inova Health System

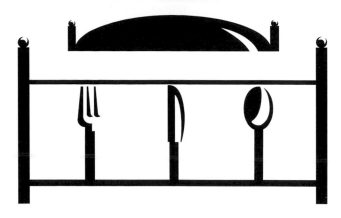

THE JIMMIE HALE MISSION

50th anniversary logo for a homeless shelter founded by a former alcoholic turned minister.

DESIGN FIRM:

Dogstar Design and Illustration, Birmingham, Alabama

ART DIRECTOR:

Ralph Watson

DESIGNER/ILLUSTRATOR:

Rodney Davidson

BUDGET: Design/paper: donated; printing: $90 (1500 business cards, envelopes and letterheads)

PRINTING PROCESS:

1-color

The logo represents the four elements of the state program providing economic development information to businesses and small towns—shopping/retail, festivals, building restoration and community involvement.

DESIGN FIRM:

Rubin Cordaro Design, Minneapolis, Minnesota

ART DIRECTOR:

Bruce Rubin

DESIGNER: J.P. Sticha

PRINTING PROCESS:

3 PMS colors, offset (brochure)

Minnesota Main Street

Marketing identity for a construction firm specializing in residential remodeling and home building. The firm follows a craftsman's approach to each job.

AGENCY:

EDS Corporate Communications, Plano, Texas

ART DIRECTOR/ DESIGNER: Gary Daniels

BUDGET: Design: $2000; printing: $3500

PRINTING PROCESS: 2/0 letterhead package

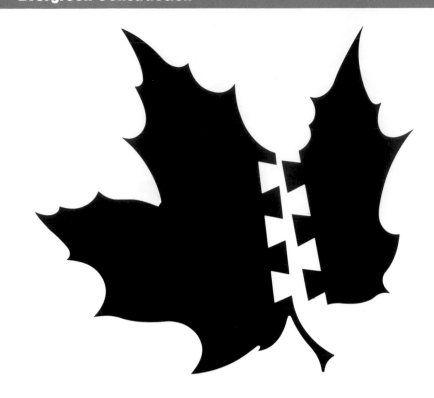

DeKalb Memorial Hospital

Promotional identity for the hospital's cardiac rehab center.

AGENCY:

Boyden & Youngblutt Advertising & Marketing, Fort Wayne, Indiana

ART DIRECTOR: Andy Boyden

DESIGNER: Don Weaver

BUDGET: Design: $2500

PRINTING PROCESS: 3-color, offset

Promotional mark for the company's interactive voice response software, Generations. The hand as a symbol represents life-giving and power, and more literally, the hand is used to press keys on a telephone keypad—both ideas relevant to the Generations software. The hieroglyphic feel provides the solid connection to the past, while the mark itself was designed to look contemporary.

DESIGN FIRM:
Stewart Monderer Design, Inc., Boston, Massachusetts
ART DIRECTOR:
Stewart Monderer
DESIGNERS:
Kathleen Smith, Stewart Monderer
BUDGET: Design: $3750 (identity)
PRINTING PROCESS:
4 match colors

Voicetek (Voicemail Software/Hardware)

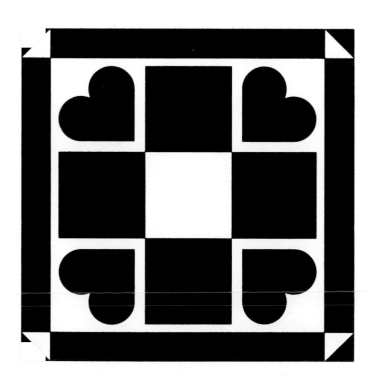

Hospice for the Heart (Home Healthcare)

Hospice works in eight rural counties in central Texas. The quilt-based design was executed in actual quilts by local women, and the quilts were sold to raise money for home care for terminally ill persons.
DESIGN FIRM:
Joseph Rattan Design, Plano, Texas
ART DIRECTOR/
DESIGNER: Joe Rattan
BUDGET: $2500
PRINTING PROCESS: Flat color, offset

Primarily a store identity, the logo was also used on a retail line of children's T-shirts and clothing and other products.

DESIGN FIRM:
William Britt Design, Princeville, Hawaii
ART DIRECTOR/
DESIGNER: William Britt
ILLUSTRATORS:
William Britt, Stephanie McFetridge Britt
PRINTING PROCESS:
4-color silkscreen (T-shirts); 2 dimensions woodcut and acrylic paint (shop signage)

Rainbow Ducks (Children's Store)

This logo was updated to include the father kangaroo when the group expanded from obstetrics/ gynecology to include other family health specialists.

DESIGN FIRM:
Evans Design Associates, Weston, Connecticut
ART DIRECTOR/
DESIGNER:
Katherine Evans
BUDGET: Design/
production: $4000;

printing: $2046 (1500 letterhead, 1000 envelopes, 7000 appointment/business cards)
PRINTING PROCESS:
2 PMS colors, offset

Associates in Family Health

Logo for an environmental fund supported by the bank.

DESIGN FIRM: Greg Welsh Design, Seattle, Washington

ART DIRECTOR/ DESIGNER: Greg Welsh

BUDGET: Design: $1500

PRINTING PROCESS: 2-color, offset (invitation only)

Puget Sound Bank

One of a number of images used as casual decorative pieces—quick, humorous thoughts to be stamped on envelopes, boxes, faxes, etc., to make recipients smile or take a second look.

DESIGN FIRM: Firehouse 101 Design, Columbus, Ohio

DESIGNER/ILLUSTRATOR: Kirk Richard Smith

BUDGET: $120 (rubber stamp series)

PRINTING PROCESS: Rubber stamp

Firehouse 101 Design (Graphic Design/Illustration)

Identity for the 1994
Colorado Bicycle tour
sponsored by the
newspaper.

DESIGN FIRM:

601 Design, Inc., Denver,
Colorado

ART DIRECTOR/

DESIGNER/ILLUSTRATOR:

Bruce Holdeman

BUDGET: Design: $7800

(logo, clothing, five 4-color

ads)

PRINTING PROCESS:

4-color, spot color

The Denver Post

Promotional identity for
a hotel restaurant.
Adaptable to 1- and 3-color
designs, the logo was used
on signage, uniforms and
advertising.

DESIGN FIRM:

Morreal Graphic Design,
San Diego, California

DESIGNER/ILLUSTRATOR:

Mary Lou Morreal

BUDGET: Design: $500

PRINTING PROCESS:

1- and 3-color, offset

Flamingo Hilton Laughlin

164

Identity for a health food/whole food market and deli reflects a casual ambience.
DESIGN FIRM:
Kenney & Westmark, Pensacola, Florida
ART DIRECTOR/
DESIGNER:
John Westmark
BUDGET: Tradeout for food

Amelia's Market & Deli

Joseph R. Thiel

The promotional logo for this illustrator/educator was done in Prismacolor on dry-wall (sheetrock).
ART DIRECTOR/
DESIGNER/ILLUSTRATOR:
Joseph R. Thiel, Sarasota, Florida
BUDGET: Printing/press type: $70
PRINTING PROCESS:
offset

DESIGN FIRM:

Garry Gates Designs,

Chatham, Massachusetts

ART DIRECTOR/

DESIGNER: Garry Gates

PRINTING PROCESS:

Silkscreen, vinyl die-cut,

offset

Cafe Kokopelli (Restaurant/Jazz Club)

DESIGN FIRM:

Pictogram Studio,

Washington, DC

ART DIRECTOR:

Stephanie Hooton

DESIGNER: Hien Nguyen

BUDGET: In trade

Barry Myers Photography (Commercial Photographer)

DESIGN FIRM:

Bernhardt Fudyma

Design Group, Inc.,

New York, New York

ART DIRECTOR:

Craig Bernhardt

DESIGNER:

Ignacio Rodriguez

BUDGET: Design:

$18,000

National Media Corporation (Infomercials/New Product Marketing)

Identity for a studio that

makes custom furniture in

Art Deco and Native

American styles.

DESIGN FIRM:

Sheriff Krebs Design,

Philadelphia, Pennsylvania

ART DIRECTORS:

Soonduk Krebs, Paul

Sheriff

DESIGNER/ILLUSTRATOR:

Soonduk Krebs

BUDGET: $2000

PRINTING PROCESS:

2-color

SB Studios (Custom Furniture)

The Atlas image is a metaphor for the film collections of Turner Entertainment Company and represents the emphasis placed on the proper storage of fragile film stockand the restoration of aging film titles.

DESIGN FIRM:
Tracy Sabin Graphic Design, San Diego, California

ART DIRECTOR:
Alison Hill
DESIGNER/ILLUSTRATOR:
Tracy Sabin

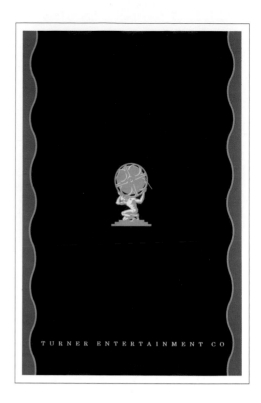

TURNER ENTERTAINMENT CO

Turner Entertainment Company (Motion Picture Film Collections)

The logo for a line of cosmetics for diabetics symbolizes the purity of the manufacturing process required by the sensitizing effects of diabetes on the skin.

DESIGN FIRM:
Love Packaging Group, Wichita, Kansas

ART DIRECTOR/
DESIGNER/ILLUSTRATOR:
Brian Miller
BUDGET: Design: $300 (logo); printing: $35 (1000 tradeshow cards)
PRINTING PROCESS:
1-color, offset

Anastasia Marie Laboratories, Inc.

This Mexican restaurant is known for its happy hour buffets. The symbol heralds the restaurant's return to traditional Mexican cuisine from a more southwestern range of food.

DESIGN FIRM: May & Co., Dallas, Texas

ART DIRECTOR: Douglas May

DESIGNER/ILLUSTRATOR: Jo Ortiz

PRINTING PROCESS: 2-color spot

Rick Mosley Hair (Hair Salon)

DESIGN FIRM: Zimmerman, Laurent & Richardson, Des Moines, Iowa

DESIGNER: Kari Clark

ACCOUNT EXECUTIVE: Louis Laurent

BUDGET: $1000

PRINTING PROCESS: Silkscreen on canvas

X Technology

Identity for a start-up
company with a name
that defines precisely (to
people in the industry)
what the company does.
DESIGN FIRM:
Sheaff Dorman Purins,
Needham, Massachusetts

ART DIRECTOR:
Uldis Purins
BUDGET: Design: $3500;
printing: $2500
PRINTING PROCESS:
4-color

Symbol for a freelance
writer reflects her
personality and her
writing—classy, creative,
unexpected.
DESIGN FIRM:
Horjus Design, San Diego,
California
DESIGNER: Peter Horjus

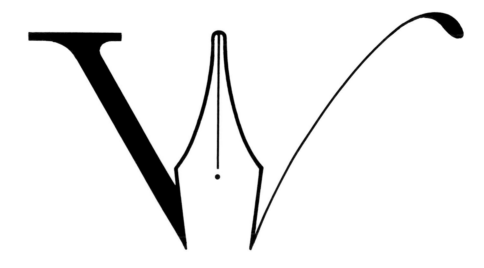

Nanette Wiser

Promotional logo for a bicycle team was applied to team members' racing jerseys.

DESIGN FIRM:

Hornall Anderson Design Works, Seattle, Washington

ART DIRECTOR:

Jack Anderson

DESIGNERS:

Jack Anderson, Brian O'Neill

V. Allen Crawford

This graphic designer/illustrator's initials form a stylized pencil or stylus, and the rays coming off the pencil symbolize inspiration.

DESIGN FIRM:

V. Allen Crawford Design, New Egypt, New Jersey

ART DIRECTOR/DESIGNER:

V. Allen Crawford

PRINTING PROCESS:

Various: laser print, silkscreen, 2-color offset

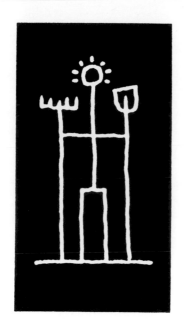

DESIGN FIRM:

Jon Flaming Design,

Dallas, Texas

ART DIRECTOR/

DESIGNER/ILLUSTRATOR:

Jon Flaming

BUDGET: Pro bono

PRINTING PROCESS:

Photocopied

S O N N Y'S

Sonny's (Architectural Landscaping)

Most applications of this logo

for an alternative rock music

label are low-resolution,

including screenprinting and

photocopied flyers, so the

image had to reproduce well

under adverse conditions.

DESIGN FIRM:

Tracy Sabin Graphic Design,

San Diego, California

ART DIRECTOR: Eero Sabin

DESIGNER/ILLUSTRATOR:

Tracy Sabin

BUDGET: Donated—

designer's son is a partner

PRINTING PROCESS:

Silkscreen (CD, T-shirt);

offset (printed materials)

Big Weenie Records

Symbol represents the solid, professional approach of these lawyers dedicated to defending the rights of their clients.

DESIGN FIRM:

John Ryan Company, Minneapolis, Minnesota

ART DIRECTOR:

Jon Trettel

DESIGNER/ILLUSTRATOR:

Scott Thares

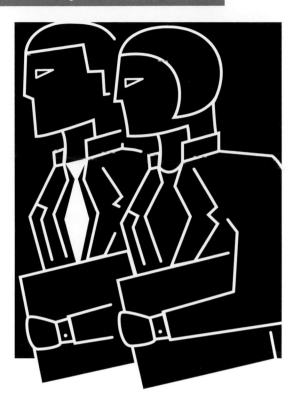

Columbus Symphony Orchestra

Logo for a series of children's outdoor symphonic concerts. The kids and their families picnic on the grass while the orchestra performs. Since introducing the logo and the picnic with the Pops theme, the concerts have been near sell-outs.

DESIGN FIRM:

New Idea Design, Inc., Omaha, Nebraska

DESIGNER/ILLUSTRATOR:

Ron Boldt

PRINTING PROCESS:

5-color, offset (print collateral), 5-color, silkscreen (garments)

The wet/dry (amphibious) uses of this clothing are indicated by the frog image created by the customized letters.

DESIGN FIRM: The Kottler Caldera Group, Phoenix, Arizona

BUDGET: Design: $15,000; production: $12,000; printing: $12,000

PRINTING PROCESS: 5/5 sheet-fed printing

Frogskin, Inc. (Sun Protective/Amphibious Children's Apparel)

THE ASIAN AND AFRICAN RAINFOREST HABITAT • CINCINNATI ZOO AND BOTANICAL GARDEN •

JUNGLE TRAILS

Logo was used to correlate the sense of immersion, interactivity, and up-closeness a new exhibit brought to visitors.

AGENCY: Mann Bukvic Associates, Cincinnati, Ohio

CREATIVE DIRECTOR: David S. Bukvic

DESIGNER: Teresa Newberry

CALLIGRAPHER: Juana Silcox

ILLUSTRATOR: Michael Halbert

BUDGET: $11,835 (presskit); $7934 (gate handout); $450 (mobile); $21,989 (TV)

The Cincinnati Zoo

The Walker Group consists of three divisions—infloor conduit, above ceiling flexible conduit and communication distribution systems. A lighting bolt serves as a unifying element representing electricity and communication and each division is depicted by an animal—bull-strength of infloor conduit, snake-flexible conduit, eagle-fast distribution.

DESIGN FIRM:

Rickabaugh Graphics, Gahanna, Ohio

ART DIRECTOR:

Eric Rickabaugh

DESIGNERS:

Eric Rickabaugh, Michael Tennyson Smith

BUDGET: $2000 (logos)

Logo announces the addition of a farmers' market to an urban area.

DESIGN FIRM:

Gardner + Greteman, Wichita, Kansas

ART DIRECTORS/

DESIGNERS: Bill Gardner, Sonia Greteman

ILLUSTRATOR:

Dave LaFleur

BUDGET: $1500

PRINTING PROCESS:

2-color

Wichita Farm & Art Market

DESIGN FIRM:

Klundt & Hosmer Design

Association, Spokane,

Washington

ART DIRECTOR:

Darin Klundt

DESIGNERS: Darin Klundt,

Rick Hosmer

ILLUSTRATOR:

Brian Gage

Land Expressions (Landscape and Water Feature Design/Construction)

M E T R O W E S T

Metrowest (Lawn Service)

Logo identifies Metrowest

as a professional, full-

service lawn company.

DESIGN FIRM:

Sullivan Perkins, Dallas,

Texas

ART DIRECTORS:

Art Garcia, Ron Sullivan

DESIGNER: Art Garcia

PRINTING PROCESS:

Offset printing for

business cards

Todd Piper-Hauswirth (Graphic Designer)

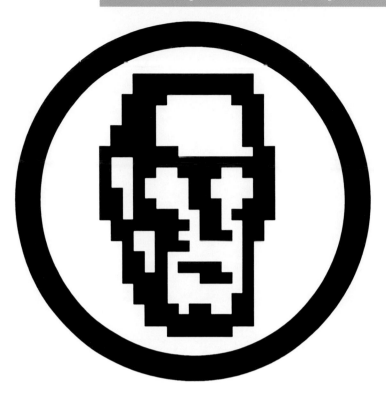

Self-promotional identity, shown very small on design projects and computer screens.

DESIGN FIRM:

C. S. Anderson Design Co., Minneapolis, Minnesota

ART DIRECTOR/

DESIGNER/ILLUSTRATOR:

Todd Piper-Hauswirth

Eagle Technology (Computer Network Hardware)

Trade show symbol provides a dynamic depiction of the company's commitment to trouble-free networking. The superhero motif communicates both a dominant presence and a dedication to solving problems. The symbol appeared on trade show announcements, T-shirts and tent cards, and on the booth itself.

DESIGN FIRM:

Energy Energy Design, Campbell, California

ART DIRECTOR/

DESIGNER/ILLUSTRATOR:

Leslie Guidice

177

This identity for the band WOWBOBWOW is playful but strong. To control costs, the logo was designed to reproduce well in 1-color and when it is photocopied.

DESIGN FIRM: Richard Leeds Design, San Mateo, California

ART DIRECTOR: Richard Leeds

DESIGNERS: Richard Leeds, Sam Miranda

BUDGET: Design: $300

PRINTING PROCESS: Photocopying and 1-color quick printing

WOWBOBWOW (Alternative Rock Band)

This logo for a sales division depicts movement and color and how they link together to form one entity.

DESIGN FIRM: West Coast Beauty Supply Co., San Francisco, California

DESIGNER: Maurice D. Thompson

West Coast Beauty Supply Company

A clean, colorful logo counteracts the dirty image normally associated with this industry.

DESIGN FIRM:

Rod Brown Design, Richardson, Texas

DESIGNER: Rod C. Brown

BUDGET: Design/ printing: $24,000

PRINTING PROCESS:

4-color

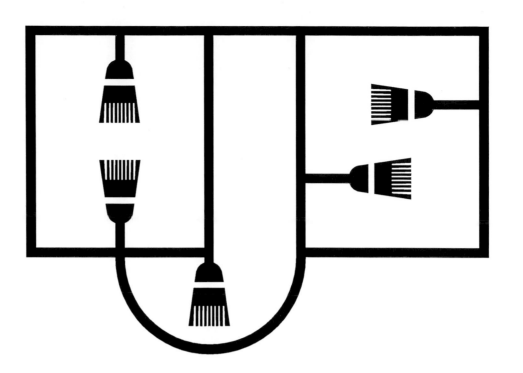

Huff Janitorial Services (Professional Commercial Cleaning Services)

The corporate identity for this international environmental clean-up group is easily recognized and understood. It appears on all collateral material, T-shirts, hard hats, etc.

DESIGN FIRM: Studio T, Clifton, New Jersey

ART DIRECTOR:

Teresa Demetriou

PRINTING PROCESS:

3 PMS colors (logo); 4 spot colors: 3PMS + black, offset (stationery)

Oasis Project

MadinaBeitia Art & Design

DESIGN FIRM:

MadinaBeitia Art & Design,

Centreville, Delaware

ART DIRECTOR/

DESIGNER:

Michele MadinaBeitia

BUDGET: Design: $650;

printing: $1582

PRINTING PROCESS:

5-color engraved printing

These self-promotional logos are meant to encourage clients to think, seek information and communicate in their role as client and partner in communication design. The logos were used on a variety of printed materials and premium items.

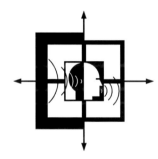

DESIGN FIRM:

THOM & DAVE Marketing Design, Media, Pennsylvania

ART DIRECTOR:

Thom Holden

DESIGNER: Dave Bell

ILLUSTRATORS: Gins, Dave Bell

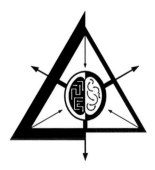

THOM & DAVE Marketing Design

Promotional logo for the 20th anniversary of an annual fundraiser for the institute.

DESIGN FIRM:
Graphic Design Continuum, Dayton, Ohio

ART DIRECTOR/
DESIGNER: John Emery

BUDGET: Pro bono

PRINTING PROCESS:
1- and 2-color offset, 1-color silkscreen, clay embossing

Two advertising agencies combined to form this limited-liability company. The spiral element that appeared in one of the agency's former logos was retained for consistency.

AGENCY:
Gunter Advertising Design, Urbandale, Iowa

ART DIRECTOR/
DESIGNER: Randy Gunter

BUDGET: Design: $0; printing. less than $200

PRINTING PROCESS:
1-color, thermography

GUNTER/WEBSTER

A handrawn logotype was created for signage purposes, and an emblem was developed for use on bread bags and labels.

DESIGN FIRM: Tharp Did It!, Los Gatos, California

ART DIRECTOR: Rick Tharp

DESIGNERS: Rick Tharp, Jean Mogannam, Jana Heer

LeBoulanger Bakeries (Bakery/Cafes in Northern California)

Logo identifies Healthpay as experts in electronic healthcare filing by combining the elements of finance, healthcare and electronics in a single mark—the medical cross combined with dollar signs, and horizontal rules suggesting an electronic screen.

DESIGN FIRM: Disciple Design & Advertising, Memphis, Tennessee

ART DIRECTOR/ DESIGNER: Craig Thompson

ILLUSTRATORS: Craig Thompson, David Terry

BUDGET: Design: $750 + expenses includes stats and filmwork (logo), $300 (letterhead); printing: $1200

PRINTING PROCESS: 2 match PMS + 5% screen of a PMS match, offset

Healthpay, Inc.

DESIGN FIRM:

Frank C. Lionetti Design, Inc,

Old Greenwich, Connecticut

ART DIRECTOR:

Frank C. Lionetti

DESIGNER: Laurie Frick

BUDGET: Design: $2900;

printing: $800

PRINTING PROCESS:

2 PMS colors

New England Adjusters (Disaster Claims Adjuster)

David Zagorski Restoration (Repair/Restoration of Art Objects)

The wavy line background was hand-drawn line art using a cardboard template. It was then shot as line film, then diffused and shot on black-and-white 35mm, then enlarged to a glossy 8x10 print, and finally shot in halftone.

DESIGN FIRM. Opal Arts, Chicago, Illinois

DESIGNER: Scott Wampler

BUDGET: Design/printing: $1000 (greater part being the printing costs—deep discount for a friend)

PRINTING PROCESS: 2-color, offset

Identity for a retirement community for the armed forces combines homes and the U.S. flag.

DESIGN FIRM:

Martin Stevers Design, Encinitas, California

ART DIRECTOR/

DESIGNER/ILLUSTRATOR:

Martin Stevers

BUDGET: Design: $1000

PRINTING PROCESS:

4-color

Armed Forces Retirement Communities

Logo for a housing development of townhomes with white stucco walls and red tile roofs in a tropical setting.

DESIGN FIRM:

Mires Design, San Diego, California

ART DIRECTOR:

Scott Mires

ILLUSTRATOR: Tracy Sabin

BUDGET: Design: $700

McMillan Communities

Logo for an in-house sales

promotion campaign.

DESIGN FIRM:

Smit Ghormley Lofgreen,

Phoenix, Arizona

ART DIRECTOR/

DESIGNER: Art Lofgreen

BUDGET: $7000

INTEL Corporation (Computers/Electronics)

Logo creates a strong
identity for Paracelsian's
product packaging and
print media within the
scientific community.

DESIGN FIRM:

Media Services, Cornell

University, Ithaca,

New York

ART DIRECTOR:

Linda Haylor-Mikula

DESIGNER:

Wendy Kenigsberg

PRODUCTION

COORDINATOR:

Donna Vantine

PRINTING PROCESS:

2 PMS colors + black

Paracelsian (Pharmaceutical/Diagnostics)

Western Exposure

Identity for Westernware product lines and consulting services.

DESIGN FIRM:

The Weller Institute for the Cure of Design, Oakley, Utah

ART DIRECTOR/ ILLUSTRATOR/DESIGNER:

Don Weller

BUDGET: Design: $1000 (logo); $500 (application); printing: $1000

PRINTING PROCESS:

2-color, offset

Symbol conveys this restaurant's unique concept: elegant dining in a restored Victorian home where all the antique furnishings—from sideboards to salad forks—are for sale. Symbol is used on menus, stationery and signage.

DESIGN FIRM:

Anne Flanagan Visual Communications, Allison Park, Pennsylvania

ART DIRECTOR/ DESIGNER/ILLUSTRATOR:

Anne Flanagan

BUDGET: Design/ production: $700 (through camera-ready art)

PRINTING PROCESS:

1-color, standard flat PMS

Cafe Victoria (Restaurant/Antique Dealer)

186

S C H W A R T Z

P H O T O G R A P H Y

Identity for a new photography studio in a saturated market. The black-and-white shapes represent the positive and negative aspects of film, while the *S* shape creates a "yin yanq" feel and draws reference to Schwartz's name.

ART DIRECTOR/
DESIGNER:Aaron Segall,
St. Louis, Missouri
BUDGET: Design: in-trade
PRINTING PROCESS:
2-color, offset

Identity logo for the 1994 shopping mall industry convention.
AGENCY:
Carmichael Lynch,
Minneapolis, Minnesota
ART DIRECTOR/
DESIGNER: Peter Winecke
ILLUSTRATOR:
Bruce Edwards
BUDGET: $1000
PRINTING PROCESS:
4-color + silkscreen

187

Design Directors/
Creative Directors/
Art Directors/Designers

Other Contributors